THE

EPISTLES OF HORACE

BOOK I.

𝕻𝖎𝖙𝖙 𝕻𝖗𝖊𝖘𝖘 𝕾𝖊𝖗𝖎𝖊𝖘.

THE

EPISTLES OF HORACE

BOOK I.

WITH INTRODUCTION AND NOTES

BY

E. S. SHUCKBURGH, M.A.

LATE FELLOW OF EMMANUEL COLLEGE.

EDITED FOR THE SYNDICS OF THE UNIVERSITY PRESS.

CAMBRIDGE:

AT THE UNIVERSITY PRESS.

1888

CAMBRIDGE UNIVERSITY PRESS
Cambridge, New York, Melbourne, Madrid, Cape Town,
Singapore, São Paulo, Delhi, Mexico City

Cambridge University Press
The Edinburgh Building, Cambridge CB2 8RU, UK

Published in the United States of America by Cambridge University Press, New York

www.cambridge.org
Information on this title: www.cambridge.org/9781107683747

First published 1888
First paperback edition 2013

A catalogue record for this publication is available from the British Library

ISBN 978-1-107-68374-7 Paperback

PREFACE.

An editor of any part of Horace takes his life in his hand. Horace has been so popular an author for so many centuries that a multitude of traditional interpretations has gathered round his text, some of which are sure to be favourites with some of his thousands of readers, who do not bear easily to have them disturbed. An editor himself is fortunate if he has not himself imbibed many prejudices as to the poet's meaning which will not stand the test of examination. For Horace is essentially one of those writers whose poems become absorbed into our thoughts and language, and his meaning is apt to suffer in the process. I can only say that I have tried to look impartially on the text of the Epistles, and to test my conception of their meaning by comparing the explanations of other editors. The text has been revised by a careful consideration of the testimony of the MSS. supplied so fully by Keller and Holder. Orelli's larger edition has been before me while I was writing my notes; which when in type I have compared with those of other editors, especially with the learned and excellent edition of my friend Professor Wilkins (1885). My own edition makes no pretension to a completeness such as his, which is a real credit to English scholarship; but though I have made some corrections in my commentary by comparing it with his, and have learned from him to modify some of my views, I have not consciously borrowed any illustrative or explanatory matter from him. Such debt as I owe to him I hope he will look upon as a homage to the excellency of his work. I have prefixed a life of Horace, which, though not pretending to give a complete abstract of what may be learnt of the poet from his own poems, may yet I hope in some degree show young readers the way to study a man's life in his works, and give a clear if only an elementary conception of his position and the order of his productiveness.

CAMBRIDGE, 1887.

INTRODUCTION.

§ 1. LIFE OF HORACE.

A WANT of adequate biographies of the men of letters in Greece and Rome is the most striking defect in ancient literature. Such as we possess are few and meagre, and fail to answer a tithe of the questions which we should be glad to put. Especially conspicuous is the absence of information as to the youth, domestic surroundings, and early training of such men. The short life of Horace which appears in the MSS. and is attributed to Suetonius does not tell us even the name of Horace's mother, or allude in any way to her. And yet the influence of a mother, or the absence of it, has often the most decisive effect upon a boy's career, especially on that of a sensitive and emotional boy such as Horace in all likelihood was. The Roman poets, notably Ovid and Horace, have however partly supplied this deficiency by numerous autobiographical allusions: and it is to our power of piecing such allusions together that we must depend principally for our knowledge of the life of our poet.

Quintus Horatius Flaccus[1] was born at Venusia [mod. Venosa] on the 8th of December B.C. 65[2]. His native town Venusia, picturesquely situated on the slopes of Mount Voltur, was on the borders of Lucania and Apulia, so that he could speak of himself as half Apulian

b. B.C. 65, Coss. L. Aurelius Cotta, L. Manlius Torquatus.

---

[1] Horace's father being a freedman the nomen Horatius, and probably the praenomen Quintus, was adopted from the patronus who had emancipated him, one of the gens Horatia, we don't know who.

[2] Sueton. Vit. Hor., cp. Ep. 1, 20, 27. Od. 3, 21, 1 *o nata mecum consule Manlio.*

half Lucanian³. It had been a town of some importance for a considerable time. A Roman colony was placed there in B.C. 262, which stood firm in its loyalty to Rome during the horrors of the Hannibalic invasion. It was then a rich town, though not protected by walls, and suffered proportionally from the wasting of its territory in B.C. 218. But it had recovered sufficiently to receive the remnants of the Roman army after Cannae [B.C. 215], supply them with food and medical treatment and with a considerable sum of money, distributed in various proportions between infantry and cavalry⁴. It had however suffered much, and in B.C. 200 its thinned ranks were supplemented by a new body of Coloni led thither by Terentius Varro, T. Quintius Flamininus, and Publius Cornelius Scipio. Thus reinforced the town once more grew in wealth and importance, and became in the Social War of B.C. 90—88 one of the strongholds of the insurgent Italian States. By the legislation which followed the Social War [*leges Iulia* and *Plauta-Papiria*] Venusia like other 'Colonies' obtained the full civitas, and in Strabo's time [about contemporary with Horace] it was still a town of importance⁵; its situation on the Via Appia contributing largely to its rapid recovery from the effects of the Social War.

In this place then, a provincial town of the better class, Quintus Horatius was born a full civis Romanus. His Father was a freedman and a collector of taxes [*exactionum exactor*]⁶. He had a small estate and house, but was by no means rich⁷; but as we shall see he took such pains and went to such expense in his son's education as to earn the boy's respect and the man's lasting gratitude.

Of Horace's early childhood we know absolutely nothing.

---

³ Sat. 2, 1, 34 *Lucanus an Apulus anceps*.
⁴ Polyb. 3, 90. Livy 22, 54; 27, 6.
⁵ πόλις ἀξιόλογος Strab. 6, 1, 3.
⁶ Sueton. Vit. Hor., cp. Sat. 1, 6, 7.
According to Suet. some declared that he was a dealer in salt fish (*salsamentarius*).
⁷ Sat. 1, 6, 71 *macro pauper agello*. Ep. 1, 20, 20 *me libertino natum patre et in tenui re.*

There is only one incident which remains embalmed in his own verses. He tell us that he once wandered in the woods of Mount Voltur which looks down upon his native Venusia, and there was found sleeping peaceably, unhurt by bear or serpent, with leaves of bay and myrtle covering him—*non sine dis animosus infans*[8]. He feigns to regard this as a presage of his coming fame; but we may dwell on it as a slightly embellished tale of a lost child, often no doubt told him by his mother who had searched for him. It is like the story related by the great-grandson of Sir Thomas More, and piously regarded as a presage of his coming sanctity. 'Once', we are told, 'his nurse riding with him in her arms across some water, the horse stumbled into a hole and put both her and the infant in great danger of drowning. To prevent this she threw the child over a hedge. By God's help escaping too she came to take the child up again expecting to find him killed or maimed, but she found him to have no hurt at all, but the babe sweetly smiled upon her[9].'

Whatever be the foundation of Horace's childish adventure he seems to have regarded it as one of the four narrow escapes, for which he had had to thank the Muses or the Gods. It is all we know of his childhood. As soon as he was old enough his father, instead of sending him to the local Day School[10] kept by one Flavius, where his schoolfellows would have been sons of centurions and the like, carried him to Rome that he might attend the best schools frequented by the sons of Equites and Senators. Horace speaks of this gratefully, as evidently an act of self-denial on his father's part, who took care that however narrow his means his boy should not be at a disadvantage in point of dress and appearance among his richer schoolmates. The wisdom of this course will perhaps be questioned by some. But those who know by experience the capacity of boys for giving pain will understand the human affection which prompted

[8] Od. 3, 4, 9—20.
[9] Life of Sir T. More, by his Great Grandson, p. 6.
[10] Like Shakespeare's schoolboy they go 'satchel on arm' and writing-tablets in hand—*laevo suspensi loculos tabulamque lacerto* (Sat. 1, 6, 74).

it. The father's care did not stop at sacrifices for the material
comfort of his boy. He gave his own time and trouble to
protect him from the moral dangers of the city, accompanying
him personally to and from his master's lecture-rooms, a duty
relegated by most fathers to the paedagogus. To this care
Horace gratefully attributes his escape from much evil: and
we feel that he is only speaking with common honesty when he
says 'may I never be ashamed of such a father[11].'

Horace had then the best education to be got at Rome.
One of the masters whose school he attended he has immortalised as *plagosus Orbilius*, being we may suppose somewhat
free in the use of the ferule. Lucius Orbilius Pupillus was a
native of Beneventum, who came to Rome in B.C. 63, when
he was 50 years old, and set up a school, after having passed his
life in various offices as apparitor and then adjutant in the army
to the Praetor. He was poor and cross-grained, and his bitter
tongue spared men as little as his pupils. Suetonius says that
he lived to be nearly a hundred[12].

Horace's elementary education being thus finished he went
? B.C. 45. to Athens, which occupied at that time the position of
an University town, to attend the lectures of the philosophers of the various sects represented there. Of the year
in which Horace arrived in Athens we have no information.
Young Cicero, the son of the Orator, who was born in the same
year as Horace, went in B.C. 45 ; and in the same year went a
young Bibulus, Acidinus, and Messalla[13] : and thus we know
four of the men, if not of Horace's year at the University, at
least of his time. The names of two of the professors also we
learn from Plutarch,—Theomnestor the Academic and Cratippus

[11] These details are all given in Sat. 1, 6, 77 sq.
[12] Suet. Grammat. § 9. Hor. Ep. 2, 1, 71. We learn also that
one of Horace's school-books from which his master dictated to him,
in order probably to learn the lines by heart, was a work of Livius
Andronicus [circ. B.C. 250].
[13] Cic. ad Att. 12, 2. We shall see presently that Horace knew
intimately two of these men in after-life, and probably therefore had
some acquaintance with them at the University, in spite of social
distinctions.

the Peripatetic, the latter of whom had received the Roman civitas by Cicero's influence[14]. What Horace did at Athens we do not know. There were the same chances of idleness and dissipation there as at modern Universities, and we know for instance that young Cicero gave his father considerable anxiety both by extravagance and wildness. We cannot imagine young Horace to have been one of the strictest of livers, but he evidently during his time there got well acquainted with Greek literature, and laid the foundation of those tastes which were afterwards to form his title to fame. It seems probable that his father was either dead when Horace went to Athens, or had died before he returned. But we are nowhere told the fact, nor do we know how long he stayed there[15]. We know however nearly when his residence came to an end. In the autumn of B.C. 44 the Praetors Brutus and Cassius parted at the Peiraeus, the latter going to Syria, the former proceeding to Athens on his way to his province of Macedonia. Brutus during his stay at Athens, which was prolonged beyond the time which his adherents thought wise, not only attended lectures of philosophers, but looked out for adherents among the students[16]. Among others the young Horace was induced to join him, and was given or quickly obtained the position of military tribune[17]. This was an absurdly high office for so young and inexperienced a man to hold ; and his appointment shows to what straits Brutus was reduced for men at that time, though he afterwards succeeded in collecting a formidable force. He contrived to annex Asia Minor to his province of Macedonia for a time, and was in various cities there in B.C. 43 and 42. And though we are not told directly that Horace accompanied

[14] Plutarch, Brut. 24. See Cic. ad Fam. 12, 16. Brut. § 250.

[15] From Ep. 2, 2, 80 (in which Horace describes a scholar spending seven years at Athens and coming out unfit for the affairs of the world) it has been thought by some that Horace spent seven years there. But Prof. Wilkins shows the groundlessness of the inference. If it had been true, Horace must have gone there in his 16th year.

[16] Plut. Brut. 24 and 28. Hor. Ep. 2, 2, 42—9.

[17] Sat. 1, 6, 48. There were six tribuni in a legion, each of which would therefore command nearly as many men as an English Lieut.-Colonel.

him, he doubtless did so. The scene in Brutus' propraetorial court at Clazomenae, described in Satire 1, 7, has all the appearance of having been witnessed by himself, and worked up into a Satiric tale[18]; and in Epistle 1, 11 he shows some detailed knowledge of Asia Minor and the adjacent islands. With Brutus Horace returned to Europe and shared in the two disasters at Philippi; and saved his life apparently by flight[19]. The two battles of Philippi, which were separated by twenty days, took place in October—November of B.C. 42. An amnesty was granted to the soldiers of the fallen regicides[20], and taking advantage of this Horace returned to Rome. But though his life was spared his father's small property was confiscated; and thus as he says, 'his wings being clipped and his father's farm and house being gone, he was compelled to throw away modesty and take to writing verses[21].' What verses he wrote and how they brought him money we are not told. We know how in later life he objected to public recitations[22]; but it does not follow that he never gave them; and long afterwards Ovid, who was born while Horace was with Brutus, heard him recite[23]. No collection of his writings was published until the first book of the Satires; and any money he may have made before by literature could hardly have been gained in any other way. But meanwhile he had other sources of livelihood. With the

B.C. 41—35.

---

[18] See Professor Palmer's introduction to Sat. 1, 7. He infers that this is Horace's earliest extant writing: and it may very likely be so, though I do not think it proved.

[19] Od. 2, 7, 9; 3, 4, 26. The *relicta non bene parmula* must not be taken too literally.

[20] τελευτήσαντος δὲ αὐτοῦ [sc. Brutus] τὸ μὲν πλῆθος τῶν στρατιωτῶν αὐτίκα ἀδείας σφίσι κηρυχθείσης μετέστη. Dio 57, 3. But it seems probable that some special act of grace relieved Horace from further consequences. The soldiers would be simply amalgamated with the victorious army. Suetonius says *venia impetrata.*

[21] Ep. 2, 2, 51—2.

[22] Ep. 1, 19, 41.

[23] Ovid, Tr. 4, 10, 49 *et tenuit nostras numerosus Horatius aures, Dum ferit Ausonia carmina culta lyra.* This must mean, looking to the context, that he had actually *heard* Horace, but whether in private or public is not so certain. Ovid was much in Society from about B.C. 20.

remnants of his fortune he purchased the position of a *scriba*, or as we should say 'a civil service clerk.' The scribae of Rome were numerous, divided into decuriae, according to the particular department to which they were attached. They were an *ordo*, that is, in our language, they had a settled precedence in the state. But though Cicero calls them an *honestus ordo*, it appears that they were to a great extent freedmen, and consequently were not regarded as holding a good social position. And in his more prosperous days Horace never mentions the fact of his having been a scriba[24].

Maecenas. B.C. 39—8. But in this period of his life another event happened to Horace which had a decisive influence on his career. In B.C. 39 or the following year he was introduced by Vergil and Varius to the great friend and minister of Augustus, Maecenas[25].

C. Cilnius Maecenas is one of the most interesting characters of the Augustan period. Without being a great soldier or a great statesman he held a commanding position at a time which seemed to especially demand both; and without any but the most mediocre powers in literature himself, habitually melancholy and valetudinarian, he yet gathered round him the gayest and brightest wits and poets in Rome. His influence with Augustus, begun it has been conjectured while the future Emperor was a boy at Apollonia, never entirely died away; and though during the last few years of his life he was treated with some coldness by the Emperor, his death was felt by the latter

[24] *Scriptum Quaestorium comparavit*, Suet. For the position see Cic. 2 Verr. 3 § 182—3. Cp. Sat. 1, 5, 65 *donasset iamne catenam ex voto Laribus, quaerebat: scriba quod esset, Nilo deterius dominae ius esse*. There appears to be an allusion to his old connection with the Scribae in Sat. 2, 6, 36 [about B.C. 31] for he is asked to come to Rome to use his influence with Maecenas on some matter affecting the *Commune Scribarum*. But Horace is evidently not proud of the position.

[25] Sat. 1, 6, 55. Vergil needs no note. For L. Varius Rufus, a poet of various styles, elegiac, epic, tragic, and Vergil's literary executor, see Ode 1, 6; Sat. 1, 10, 44; Ep. 1, 16, 27. He died some time after B.C. 19. For the beginning of Horace's intimacy with Maecenas see Sat. 2, 6, 40 written at the end of B.C. 31 or beginning of 30; where he reckons it to have lasted eight years.

as a deep sorrow[26]. He is said to have been with Augustus at
Mutina, Philippi and Perusia [43—41]: to have negociated the
peace between him and Antony in B.C. 38; and to have accompanied Augustus to Sicily in B.C. 36, from which he was sent
back as his vicegerent to Rome, and to have been entrusted
with his seal and the absolute power of dealing with all his
public despatches[27]. This position of trust and confidence he
retained until about B.C. 16. He amassed a large fortune in
the course of his service, which he dispensed with liberality
though without ostentation in his house on the Esquiline[28],
where Horace soon became a regular and favourite guest. It

38—35.   was probably in B.C. 38 that he accompanied Maecenas
on the journey to Brundisium immortalised in his Satire

Satires I.   (1, 5), and during the years which followed gradually
Epodes.   composed the poems which form the first book of
B.C. 35—30. the Satires, and the Epodes.

The Satires though not collected until B.C. 35 had been read
or listened to in detail by Horace's friends before, and Satire
I, 10 gives us the means of seeing who the chief members of
this set were. We find in the list two of those who had been
with Horace at Athens, Messalla and Bibulus; Sulpicius Rufus,
Plotius Tusca and Varius [Od. 2, 95], the editors of the Aeneid;
the poet and historian Octavius Musa; C. Furnius the orator;
C. Asinius Pollio [Od. 2, 1, 9], who was at once a soldier, orator
and poet, the founder of a public library, and the hero of a
triumphant war in Dalmatia; Aristius Fuscus (Od. 1, 22) a
poet; Maecenas his patron and constant friend, and Vergilius
to whom he owed his introduction[29]. To this list ought
perhaps to be added later the poet Propertius, who was inti-

---

   [26] *desideravit...Maecenatis taciturnitatem,* Suet. Aug. 66. The
cause of the coldness according to Suetonius was the fact that Maecenas
had betrayed to his wife Terentia some secret as to the conspiracy of
her brother Murena. Dio gives an explanation less creditable to
Augustus.
   [27] Dio 51, 3.
   [28] See Horace Sat. 1, 8, 14 *Esquiliis salubribus.* Cp. 2, 6, 33.
   [29] Hor. Sat. 1, 10, 81 sq.

mate with Maecenas, but whom Horace never mentions[30]. This was a brilliant circle for the freedman's son; and he evidently felt it to be so, and was not altogether untainted with that contempt for men of inferior rank which is apt to be the result in the mind of a man who finds himself mixing with his superiors in social position in virtue of his abilities[31].

Between the publication of these two collected works[32], he was lifted out of all danger of poverty by a gift of a small estate in the country of the Sabines, some few miles from Tivoli. The description of this property, which was large enough to maintain five tenants or coloni, is given in the 16th epistle of this book. It was in a retired valley, and seems to have been mostly agricultural and pastoral, not fitted for vines of any quality, but no doubt growing olives[33]. The poet continually refers to this spot not only as giving him the peace and health which he missed at Rome, but as securing him from all sordid care. He seems to have at once set about building himself a small house on his farm[34], and to this he retired even more often, it appears, than quite suited the taste of his patron, who lived much in Town[35], and did not easily leave his lofty palace on the Esquiline except on the Emperor's business.

Horace probably ceased on getting his Sabine farm to act as a scriba, though as far as his social rank went he was still of that ordo. But he did not cease entirely his literary activity. The second book of Satires was published about B.C. 30. Yet in the second Satire of this book he reproaches himself with idleness, and in the first he shows that he felt the enmity which his style of writing had roused

B.C. 34. (margin)

Satires,
Book II. B.C.
30, aet. 34. (margin)

[30] Some people have even supposed that he was the bore on 'the sacred way' of Sat. 1, 9; though it seems certain that this poem was written not later than B.C. 34 when Propertius was about 16. See Palmer's introduction.

[31] For instances see Ep. 1, 19, 39. Sat. 1, 5, 34—5.

[32] Epode 1, 31 is the earliest notice of the liberality of Maecenas in Horace's published work.

[33] Cp. Ep. 1, 14, 23 and 8, 5.

[34] See Sat. 2, 307 sq. written about 33 B.C.

[35] *Multum in urbe vixit* Tac. Ann. 14, 53. Cp. Hor. Ep. 1, 7.

against him. Still the fifth and seventh of this book (on 'Legacy Hunting' and on 'Vulgar ostentation in banquets') are more bitter satires than any other of his writings. The others are chiefly philosophical, reminiscences of his old Athenian studies as applied to actual life in Rome: while the sixth (on 'Country and town life') shows the effect upon him of his recently acquired ease and position as a landed proprietor.

The Epodes had been an attempt to use the Greek trimeter iambic in Latin. Horace now turned his thoughts to a more extended use of the Greek metres. The poems of the Aeolian Alcaeus and Sappho especially attracted him[36]; and the conse-

Odes, Books 1—3. B.C. 25 —4. quence was the production in the course of the next seven years of the detached poems which were collected and published in three books of Carmina in B.C. 25 or 24.

The Carmina or Odes are a collection of short lyrical poems of varying tone and on various subjects. Perhaps the prevailing theme is the praise of love and wine; but among such there are others, inspired apparently by his patron's policy, touching on public affairs, and recommending moderation and caution. The triumphant career of Augustus inspires others; and through all there is continually breaking out that note of sadness which was forced from the poet by the thought of the irresistible fate which hung over men, and the certainty of death[37]. Some time during this period occurred the second of the four escapes, which he attributed to the care of the Muses,—he was all but killed by the fall of a tree. Whether the fourth, his escape from shipwreck, may be placed in the same period we cannot determine. It appears to have happened on the 1st of March off Cape Palinurus in Lucania, on a voyage to Sicily, of which we know nothing

---

[36] Odes 3, 30, 13 *princeps Aeolium carmen ad Italos deduxisse modos.* Ep. 1, 19, 23 where the order of his Greek imitations is given, (1) the Iambics of Archilochus (Epodes), (2) the metres of Sappho and Alcaeus.

[37] For instances see Od. 1, 4; 1, 11; 1, 24; 1, 28; 2, 3; 2, 14; 2, 16; 2, 18. This is less apparent in the third book, written at a time when Horace may be regarded as perhaps at his happiest and most prosperous time.

else[38]. But we may remark that as a Quaestorian Scriba he may have had to go with a Quaestor to Sicily more than once.

Horace seems to have intended this to be the end of his literary career. But the remonstrances of Maecenas produced a collection of poems differing considerably from the Satires in tone, and differing in form in so far as they profess to be addressed directly to individuals. In some cases they are really poetical 'letters', in others they are only nominally so. Like his other works, they begin with an address to Maecenas; and appear to have been published in B.C. 19. But Horace was now to fall under another influence. We do not know exactly when he began to be intimate with Augustus. But evidently before the publication of the first book of the Epistles he had been admitted to read some of his poems to the Emperor[39]; who, according to Suetonius, offered him the post of private secretary; and bore his refusal of that exalted, though onerous, office with good temper; and pressed upon him other favours[40]. What he took we do not know, but Augustus is said to have 'twice enriched him by his liberality[41]'. The poet behaved with caution. Though he sent a copy of his Epistles to the Emperor, he did not venture to dedicate it to him, or to speak openly of his intimacy. But as the influence of Maecenas had induced him to write *Sermones* once more in B.C. 20—19, so now the influence of the Emperor turned him again to Lyrics. In B.C. 17 he was commissioned to write the ode to be performed at the Secular games; and about B.C. 12 produced at the

Epistles, Book I. 25—19.

Acquaintance with Augustus.

Carmen Saeculare, B.C. 17.

---

[38] Ode 3, 4, 29 *nec Sicula Palinurus unda.* As Cape Palinurus is not on the *Mare Siculum*, this can only mean 'on a voyage to Sicily.' Unless *Palinurus* is not the Cape at all, but used as a general name for a Steersman, and the *Sicula unda* the real mare Siculum? For the fall of the tree, see also Od. 2, 13, and 3, 8.

[39] Ep. I, 19.

[40] Suet. Vit. Hor. *Augustus epistolarum ei officium obtulit...ac ne recusanti quidem aut succensuit quicquam aut amicitiam suam ingerere desiit.*

[41] *Unaque et altera liberalitate locupletavit.* Suet.

Odes, Book IV.
B.C. 13—12.
Emperor's request the Fourth book of the Odes[42]. The object was especially to celebrate the greatness of Augustus and the achievements of his stepsons, Tiberius and Drusus. This is done in Odes 4, 5, 14, 15. The rest are slighter poems on the old theme of love; and one (7) recalling the old sadness, intensified by advancing years, caused by the thought of the inevitable end. Maecenas was now in comparative disgrace with Augustus. The book is produced at the latter's command; and naturally could not be dedicated as before to Maecenas. One allusion however[43] shows that the old intimacy was kept up, and under the circumstances may be put down to the credit of the loyalty of the poet to his patron; for his disposition, however faulty in some respects, was evidently warmly affectionate.

Epistles, Book II.
B.C. 12.
Following these were the 2nd Epistle of the 2nd book, and the Ars poetica or Epistula ad Pisones. And Augustus having complained that he was not mentioned in them, the poet published them with a preface (Epist. 2, 1) addressed directly to the Emperor[44].

B.C. 8.
This is the last that we know of Horace. He lived four more years, doubtless in comfort as far as worldly wealth was concerned, and died 8 November B.C. 8, not long after his friend and patron Maecenas: thus fulfilling his lyrical prophecy or promise (Od. 2, 17)

ille dies utramque
ducet ruinam. non ego perfidum
dixi sacramentum : ibimus, ibimus
utcunque praecedes, supremum
carpere iter comites parati.

[42] *Scripta quidem eius usque adeo probavit mansuraque perpetua opinatus est, non modo Seculare carmen componendum iniunxerit sed et Vindelicam Victoriam Tiberii Drusique, privignorum suorum, eumque coegit propter hoc tribus carminum libris ex longo intervallo quartum addere.*

[43] In which he mentions that he is keeping the birthday of Maecenas. Od. 4, 11.

[44] This seems a better account of the order of these books than to regard the *libellus* of which Augustus complained as being Satires book II.

§ 2. THE EPISTLES.

Though there may be no direct evidence that the collection of poems, which we know by the name of Epistles, was called so by Horace, yet there is very strong reason to believe it. There is almost a complete consensus of MSS. in its favour; and Horace himself speaks of Julius Florus complaining *quod epistula nulla rediret*[45], because the poet had sent no Epistle to him. This is evidently meant not of an ordinary letter, but of a composition such as Horace had addressed to others. It is true that the poet seems to include them with the Satires under the general name of *Sermones*; but that is merely in contra-distinction to lyrical carmina or to Epic poetry[46].

We may then properly call these poems *Epistulae*. But though they are all so in form, some of them are so only in form. The first, which probably was composed last to form an introduction, is rather a discursive essay, firstly on Horace's views of philosophy, and secondly on the variety of aim and character which he sees round him. The second is, like the first, only an Epistle in form, really another essay on practical philosophy suggested by a reperusal of Homer. The third, fourth and fifth are much more really Epistles, addressed as an ordinary letter might be to absent friends, though clothed in poetical garb, and again harping on his favourite ethical topics. The sixth is an essay again, merely colourably addressed to an individual. The seventh is a sort of *apologia* of the poet's, addressed to Maecenas, and laying down the terms by which he means to be bound in his relationship to him. The eighth, ninth, less emphatically the tenth, the eleventh, twelfth, are real letters: the ninth a very carefully worded one, introducing a friend to Tiberius. The thirteenth, under cover of a letter of directions to the bearer of his book, is a cautious intimation of its being forwarded early for the Emperor's perusal. The fourteenth is probably, as far as its address goes, wholly imaginary. The fifteenth seems again a real letter of enquiry.

[45] Ep. 2, 2, 22.
[46] See for a definition of *Sermo* Sat. 1, 4, 39—48. Cp. Ep. 2, 1, 251.

The sixteenth a pleasant description of his country life, with reflections, thrown into the form of a letter. The seventeenth, eighteenth and nineteenth seem to me to most nearly approach Satires, though there are probably personal hints affecting the persons addressed which justify their being included under the head of Epistles. The twentieth and last is an epilogue to the book.

Thus the poems of this collection are not all Epistles in the same sense. But they have this feature in common, that they all have some, although in certain of them brief and unimportant, personal allusions ; and that being nominally addressed (except the twentieth and\perhaps the fourteenth) to a definite individual they were probably sent to him before recitation to others, or ultimate publication.

As to their date, they seem to range from B.C. 21 to 19. Though 12, 27 seems to point to B.C. 20 as the date of publication, when Horace may have said that he completed his forty-fourth year in December of the year of Lollius [B.C. 21] : yet it would be possible to use the expression a year later; and I cannot believe that 12, 26 was written until B.C. 19, for in no sense could the Cantabrian be said to have 'fallen' until the campaign of B.C. 19.

§ 3. THE PERSONS ADDRESSED.

Epistles 1, 7, 19 are addressed to Maecenas, the first as a compliment, the seventh as a sort of manifesto, the nineteenth as the natural person to whom the poet would appeal in a personal difficulty. Of his political position enough has been said in the life of Horace. Though exercising the highest authority under Augustus he accepted no magistracy, and remained an eques [Od. 1, 20, 5 *care Maecenas eques*]. Many things endeared him to Horace besides his munificence ; and perhaps most of all his sympathy with learning and his taste in literature. Thus in Ep. 19 he addresses him as *docte*, which generally referred to a knowledge of Greek, just as in Od. 3, 8,

5 he addresses him as *docte sermones utriusque linguae.* He is his *praesidium et dulce decus* (Od. 1, 1), his *columen rerum* (2, 16, 4), the glory of the Equites (3, 16, 20). He tries to coax him away from too anxious a care for state affairs (3, 29), and to the last keeps his birthday (on the Ides of April, Od. 4, 11, 15).

Epistles 2 and 18 are addressed to Lollius Maximus, probably a son of M. Lollius, addressed in Ode 4, 9, who died in the East about the time of the Christian Era. The father was in high favour with Augustus ; and the son of whom we know nothing else beyond what we learn from these two Epistles had also served under Augustus in Spain (18, 55) in B.C. 26.

Epistle 3 is addressed to Julius Florus, to whom also Ep. 2, 2 is addressed. He appears to have been a writer of satires, some adapted from the old writers Ennius, Lucilius, and Varro. Beyond this and the fact here alluded to that he served in the East with Tiberius, we know nothing of him.

Epistle 4 is addressed to Albius Tibullus. The date of his birth is doubtful, between B.C. 59—4. He died soon after Vergil [B.C. 19]. Thus Ovid, who was born in B.C. 43, says *' Vergilium vidi tantum : nec amara Tibullo Tempus amicitiae fata dedere meae'* [Tristia 4, 10, 51]. Tibullus had a small estate near Pedum, between Praeneste and Tibur, which had been much curtailed by the confiscations [El. 1, 1, 19—20], but he lived contentedly on the remainder, and was apparently, from his own poems, as gentle and retiring as we should gather from the tone of Horace's letter to him. See also Ode 1, 33 addressed to him.

Epistle 5. Addressed to Torquatus, who is alluded to in Odes 4, 7, 23, as a man of eloquence and goodness ; but we have no means of identifying him.

Ep. 6 to Numicius, also an unknown person.

Epistle 8 to Celsus Albinovanus, see Ep. 1, 3, 15, from which it appears that he too was on the staff of Tiberius in the East. But we know nothing more of him.

Ep. 9 to Septimius, the devoted friend of Od. 2, 6 *Septimi Gades aditure mecum.* He is identified by the Scholiast probably without reason with Titius, cf. 3, 9. He was also a friend of Augustus, and is mentioned by him in a letter to Horace. Suet. Vit. Hor.

Ep. 10 to Aristius Fuscus, to whom is addressed the charming Ode *Integer vitae* (1, 22), and who left the poet in the lurch under the hands of the bore (Sat. 1, 9, 61). The old commentators say that he wrote Tragedies, and an address to Pollio. He is counted among Horace's set in Sat. 1, 10, 83.

Ep. 11 to Bullatius, an unknown person.

Ep. 12 to Iccius of Ode 1, 29, where his intended journey in Arabia in the expedition of Aelius Gallus [B.C. 25] is alluded to. That and the fact of his having now become the procurator of Agrippa in Sicily is all we know of him.

Ep. 13 to Vinius, an unknown man, if indeed it is not a fictitious name altogether.

Ep. 14 to Horace's farm bailiff, unnamed.

Ep. 15 to C. Numonius Vala, an unknown man.

Ep. 16 to Quinctius Hirpinus of Ode 2, 11, from which he appears to have been engaged in active politics, but we know nothing more of him. Professor Wilkins thinks he is the T. Quinctius Hirpinus who was Consul in B.C. 9.

Ep. 17. Scaeva or Lollius Scaeva, of whom we know nothing except that the Scholiasts call him a Roman knight. It seems possible that in this case too the name is wholly fictitious.

The general result is that as far as the persons selected by Horace to be addressed can be identified they may be said to have been men of high social rank, or men known for literary ability : exactly the set which the list of Satire 1, 10 describes.

Q. HORATI FLACCI
EPISTVLARVM

LIBER PRIMVS.

I.

TO MAECENAS.

I shall always be a grateful admirer of yours, Maecenas; but
you must not ask me for poetry of the old playful kind.
I am getting old, and am now studying philosophy.

Prima dicte mihi, summa dicende Camena,
spectatum satis et donatum iam rude quaeris,
Maecenas, iterum antiquo me includere ludo?
non eademst aetas, non mens. Veianius armis
Herculis ad postem fixis latet abditus agro,   5
ne populum extrema totiens exoret arena.
Est mihi purgatam crebro qui personet aurem:
'solve senescentem mature sanus equum, ne
peccet ad extremum ridendus et ilia ducat.'
Nunc itaque et versus et cetera ludicra pono   10
quid verum atque decens curo et rogo. et omnis in hoc
    sum;
condo et conpono quae mox depromere possim.

What school of philosophy have I joined? None absolutely.
I am an eclectic: sometimes I am for the active life of the
Stoics; at others insensibly slip back into the pursuit of
personal happiness recommended by the Cyrenaics: and I
am impatient to carry out my lessons.

Ac ne forte roges, quo me duce, quo lare tuter:
nullius addictus iurare in verba magistri

quo me cumque rapit tempestas, deferor hospes :   15
nunc agilis fio et mersor civilibus undis,
virtutis verae custos rigidusque satelles ;
nunc in Aristippi furtim praecepta relabor,
et mihi res, non me rebus subiungere conor.
Vt nox longa quibus mentitur amica, diesque   20
longa videtur opus debentibus, ut piger annus
pupillis, quos dura premit custodia matrum,
sic mihi tarda fluunt ingrataque tempora, quae spem
consiliumque morantur agendi naviter id quod
aeque pauperibus prodest, locupletibus aeque,   25
aeque neglectum pueris senibusque nocebit.

I am however content with a very moderate proficiency. It is
something to have learnt to control the grosser passions.
Negative virtues are better than none. Men will do any-
thing to avoid poverty and failure, why not to avoid vice?
This is surely a higher object.

Restat, ut his ego me ipse regam solerque elementis.
Non possis oculo quantum contendere Lynceus :
non tamen idcirco contemnas lippus inungui ;
nec, quia desperes invicti membra Glyconis,   30
nodosa corpus nolis prohibere cheragra :
est quadam prodire tenus, si non datur ultra.
Fervet avaritia miseroque cupidine pectus :
sunt verba et voces, quibus hunc lenire dolorem
possis et magnam morbi deponere partem.   35
Laudis amore tumes : sunt certa piacula, quae te
ter pure lecto poterunt recreare libello.
Invidus, iracundus, iners, vinosus, amator,
nemo adeo ferus est, ut non mitescere possit,
si modo culturae patientem commodet aurem.   40
Virtus est vitium fugere et sapientia prima

stultitia caruisse.   Vides, quae maxima credis
esse mala, exiguum censum turpemque repulsam,
quanto devites animi capitisque labore ;
inpiger extremos curris mercator ad Indos,   45
per mare pauperiem fugiens, per saxa, per ignes :
ne cures ea, quae stulte miraris et optas,
discere et audire et meliori credere non vis?
quis circum pagos et circum compita pugnax
magna coronari contemnat Olympia, cui spes,   50
cui sit condicio dulcis sine pulvere palmae?
vilius argentumst auro, virtutibus aurum.

But money, money is the cry from old and young.   Yet boys in
their games go by merit; and you will find that a good con-
science is better than wealth.

'O cives, cives, quaerenda pecunia primumst ;
virtus post nummos !' haec Ianus summus ab imo
prodocet, haec recinunt iuvenes dictata senesque   55
laevo suspensi loculos tabulamque lacerto.
Est animus tibi, sunt mores, est lingua fidesque,
sed quadringentis sex septem milia desunt :
plebs eris.   At pueri ludentes 'rex eris' aiunt
'si recte facies.'   Hic murus aheneus esto,   60
nil conscire sibi, nulla pallescere culpa.
Roscia, dic sodes, melior lex an puerorumst
nenia, quae regnum recte facientibus offert,
et maribus Curiis et decantata Camillis?
isne tibi melius suadet, qui rem facias, rem,   65
si possis, recte, si non, quocumque modo rem,
ut propius spectes lacrimosa poemata Pupi;
an qui Fortunae te responsare superbae
liberum et erectum praesens hortatur et aptat?

Why not take the popular view? say people.   But what is it? I
reply.   Tastes differ; and even in those tastes men are con-
stantly changing: Baiae to-day, Teanum to-morrow for my
Lord; a change of garrets or barbers for the needy.

Quodsi me populus Romanus forte roget, cur   70
non ut porticibus sic iudiciis fruar isdem,
nec sequar aut fugiam quae diligit ipse vel odit,
olim quod volpes aegroto cauta leoni
respondit, referam: 'quia me vestigia terrent,
omnia te adversum spectantia, nulla retrorsum.'   75
Belua multorum es capitum: nam quid sequar aut quem?
pars hominum gestit conducere publica; sunt qui
frustis et pomis viduas venentur avaras,
excipiantque senes, quos in vivaria mittant;
multis occulto crescit res fenore.   Verum   80
esto aliis alios rebus studiisque teneri:
idem eadem possunt horam durare probantes?
'nullus in orbe sinus Bais praelucet amoenis'
si dixit dives, lacus et mare sentit amorem
festinantis eri; cui si vitiosa libido   85
fecerit auspicium, 'cras ferramenta Teanum
tolletis, fabri.'   Lectus genialis in aulast:
nil ait esse prius, melius nil caelibe vita;
si non est, iurat bene solis esse maritis.
Quo teneam vultus mutantem Protea nodo?   90
quid pauper? ride: mutat cenacula, lectos,
balnea, tonsores, conducto navigio aeque
nauseat ac locuples quem ducit priva triremis.

A fantastic incongruity in dress or personal appearance would
make you think me mad.   Why not such capricious change-
ableness?

Si curatus inaequali tonsore capillos

occurri, rides : si forte subucula pexae   95
trita subest tunicae, vel si toga dissidet inpar,
rides : quid? mea cum pugnat sententia secum,
quod petiit spernit, repetit quod nuper omisit,
aestuat et vitae disconvenit ordine toto,
diruit, aedificat, mutat quadrata rotundis?   100
insanire putas sollemnia me neque rides,
nec medici credis nec curatoris egere
a praetore dati, rerum tutela mearum
cum sis et prave sectum stomacheris ob unguem
de te pendentis, te respicientis amici.   105

In fact the only great and sound man is the Philosopher,—unless
he have a cold.

Ad summam : sapiens uno minor est Iove, dives,
liber, honoratus, pulcher, rex denique regum,
praecipue sanus, nisi cum pituita molestast.

II.

TO LOLLIUS.

I have been reading Homer : he is the best of moral teachers,
for he teaches by examples.

Troiani belli scriptorem, Maxime Lolli,
dum tu declamas Romae, Praeneste relegi,
qui, quid sit pulchrum, quid turpe, quid utile, quid non,
planius ac melius Chrysippo et Crantore dicit.
Cur ita crediderim, nisi quid te detinet, audi.   5

*Paris. Wilful profligacy involving nations in war, which will
sacrifice even life to desire.*

Fabula, qua Paridis propter narratur amorem
Graecia barbariae lento collisa duello,
stultorum regum et populorum continet aestus.
Antenor censet belli praecidere causam :
quid Paris ? ut salvus regnet vivatque beatus,   10
cogi posse negat.

*Agamemnon and Achilles. Desire and anger blind them to
reason. The people have to pay for their leaders' follies: in
and out of Troy there are the miseries arising from selfish
crimes.*

                    Nestor conponere lites
inter Peliden festinat et inter Atriden :
hunc amor, ira quidem communiter urit utrumque.
Quidquid delirant reges, plectuntur Achivi :
seditione, dolis, scelere atque libidine et ira   15
Iliacos intra muros peccatur et extra.

*The reverse picture is that of Ulysses. His wisdom and self-
control succeed when passion, greed, and folly fail.*

Rursus, quid virtus et quid sapientia possit,
utile proposuit nobis exemplar Vlixen,
qui domitor Troiae multorum providus urbes
et mores hominum inspexit, latumque per aequor,   20
dum sibi, dum sociis reditum parat, aspera multa
pertulit, adversis rerum inmersabilis undis.
Sirenum voces et Circae pocula nosti ;
quae si cum sociis stultus cupidusque bibisset,
sub domina meretrice fuisset turpis et excors,   25
vixisset canis inmundus vel amica luto sus.

*The Suitors. A picture of idle youth; whose idea of 'life' was
    sleep till noonday, gay dress, wanton music.*

Nos numerus sumus et fruges consumere nati,
sponsi Penelopae, nebulones, Alcinoique
in cute curanda plus aequo operata iuventus,
cui pulchrum fuit in medios dormire dies et   30
ad strepitum citharae cessatum ducere curam.

*Every object which men care to attain they will take pains to
    get. Neglect of proper means involves failure. So it is with
    the mind. To put off moral reform is to act like the rustic
    waiting for the stream to flow by.*

Vt iugulent hominem, surgunt de nocte latrones:
ut te ipsum serves, non expergisceris? atqui
si noles sanus, curres hydropicus; et ni
posces ante diem librum cum lumine, si non   35
intendes animum studiis et rebus honestis,
invidia vel amore vigil torquebere. Nam cur
quae laedunt oculum festinas demere; siquid
est animum, differs curandi tempus in annum?
dimidium facti, qui coepit, habet: sapere aude: 40
incipe: qui recte vivendi prorogat horam,
rusticus exspectat dum defluat amnis; at ille
labitur et labetur in omne volubilis aevum.

*We are always seeking fresh sources of pleasure; but happi-
    ness consists not of things to enjoy, but in the power to enjoy
    them. Wealth to the mind racked with care is as music to
    the deaf. The vessel must be clean or the wine turns sour.*

Quaeritur argentum puerisque beata creandis
uxor, et incultae pacantur vomere silvae: 45
quod satis est cui contingit, nihil amplius optet.
Non domus et fundus, non aeris acervus et auri

aegroto domini deduxit corpore febres,
non animo curas : valeat possessor oportet,
si conportatis rebus bene cogitat uti.   50
Qui cupit aut metuit, iuvat illum sic domus et res,
ut lippum pictae tabulæ, fomenta podagrum,
auriculas citharae collecta sorde dolentes.
Sincerumst nisi vas, quodcumque infundis acescit.

Vicious pleasures bring their own punishment, notably the short madness called anger.

Sperne voluptates : nocet empta dolore voluptas.   55
Semper avarus eget : certum voto pete finem.
Invidus alterius macrescit rebus opimis ;
invidia Siculi non invenere tyranni
maius tormentum.   Qui non moderabitur irae,
infectum volet esse, dolor quod suaserit et mens,   60
dum poenas odio per vim festinat inulto.
Ira furor brevis est : animum rege ; qui nisi paret,
imperat : hunc frenis, hunc tu conpesce catena.

The only cure for these is early and constant training, 'ohne Hast ohne Rast.'

Fingit equum tenera docilem cervice magister
ire viam qua monstret eques ; venaticus, ex quo   65
tempore cervinam pellem latravit in aula,
militat in silvis catulus.   Nunc adbibe puro
pectore verba puer, nunc te melioribus offer :
quo semel est imbuta recens servabit odorem
testa diu.   Quodsi cessas aut strenuus anteis,   70
nec tardum opperior nec praecedentibus insto.

III.

TO JULIUS FLORUS.

*I want to hear from you, Florus, where you are, and where the
Prince is.*

Iuli Flore, quibus terrarum militet oris
Claudius Augusti privignus, scire laboro.
Thracane vos Hebrusque nivali compede vinctus,
an freta vicinas inter currentia turres,
an pingues Asiae campi collesque morantur?   5

*The staff is a party of scholars; what are they writing? Is it
history or lyric poetry?*

Quid studiosa cohors operum struit? hoc quoque curo:
quis sibi res gestas Augusti scribere sumit?
bella quis et paces longum diffundit in aevum?
quid Titius Romana brevi venturus in ora,
Pindarici fontis qui non expalluit haustus,   10
fastidire lacus et rivos ausus apertos?
ut valet? ut meminit nostri? fidibusne Latinis
Thebanos aptare modos studet auspice Musa,
an tragica desaevit et ampullatur in arte?

*Admonish Celsus to depend more on his own genius, and less on
that of others.*

quid mihi Celsus agit? monitus multumque monendus,   15
privatas ut quaerat opes et tangere vitet
scripta, Palatinus quaecumque recepit Apollo,
ne, si forte suas repetitum venerit olim
grex avium plumas, moveat cornicula risum
furtivis nudata coloribus.

S. H.   3

*Especially what are you doing yourself? You can succeed in
anything you try; but if you will take my advice you will
devote yourself to philosophy : there is the secret of usefulness
and happiness.*

              Ipse quid audes?   20
quae circumvolitas agilis thyma? Non tibi parvum
ingenium, non incultumst et turpiter hirtum :
seu linguam causis acuis seu civica iura
respondere paras seu condis amabile carmen,
prima feres hederae victricis praemia. Quodsi   25
frigida curarum fomenta relinquere posses,
quo te caelestis sapientia duceret, ires.
Hoc opus, hoc studium parvi properemus et ampli,
si patriae volumus, si nobis vivere cari.

*Don't quarrel with Munatius; you are both too good, and I am
eager to welcome both home.*

Debes hoc etiam rescribere, sit tibi curae   30
quantae conveniat Munatius : an male sarta
gratia nequiquam coit et rescinditur, ac vos
seu calidus sanguis seu rerum inscitia vexat
indomita cervice feros? Vbicumque locorum
vivitis, indigni fraternum rumpere foedus,   35
pascitur in vestrum reditum votiva iuvenca.

IV.

TO ALBIUS TIBULLUS, THE POET.

*What is my friendly critic Albius doing in the country? Some-
thing worthy of the good and wise man, I am sure.*

Albi, nostrorum sermonum candide iudex,
quid nunc te dicam facere in regione Pedana?

scribere quod Cassi Parmensis opuscula vincat,
an tacitum silvas inter reptare salubres,
curantem quidquid dignum sapiente bonoquest ?   5
non tu corpus eras sine pectore : di tibi formam,
di tibi divitias dederunt artemque fruendi.
Quid voveat dulci nutricula maius alumno,
qui sapere et fari possit quae sentiat, et cui
gratia, fama, valetudo contingat abunde,   10
et mundus victus non deficiente crumena ?

*Only remember the uncertainty of life, and make the best of the
present; you will find me ready to do so with you.*

Inter spem curamque, timores inter et iras
omnem crede diem tibi diluxisse supremum :
grata superveniet, quae non sperabitur hora.
Me pinguem et nitidum bene curata cute vises,   15
cum ridere voles Epicuri de grege porcum.

V.

AN INVITATION TO A FRIEND.

*If you can put up with simple fare and a plain room I shall
expect you this evening. If you want better wine than mine
bring or order it.*

Si potes Archiacis conviva recumbere lectis
nec modica cenare times olus omne patella,
supremo te sole domi, Torquate, manebo.
Vina bibes iterum Tauro diffusa palustres
inter Minturnas Sinuessanumque Petrinum :   5
si melius quid habes, arcesse vel imperium fer.

All is ready: away with work: 'tis Caesar's birthday, and a
time for mirth.   Over-stinginess is folly; and wine opens
and warms the heart.

Iamdudum splendet focus et tibi munda supellex:
mitte leves spes et certamina divitiarum
et Moschi causam: cras nato Caesare festus
dat veniam somnumque dies, inpune licebit   10
aestivam sermone benigno tendere noctem.
Quo mihi fortunam, si non conceditur uti?
parcus ob heredis curam nimiumque severus
adsidet insano: potare et spargere flores
incipiam patiarque vel inconsultus haberi.   15
Quid non ebrietas dissignat? operta recludit,
spes iubet esse ratas, ad proelia trudit inertem,
sollicitis animis onus eximit, addocet artes.
Fecundi calices quem non fecere disertum?
contracta quem non in paupertate solutum?   20

I will see that everything is clean and bright, and the company
to your taste: and you shall settle the number yourself.

Haec ego procurare et idoneus imperor et non
invitus, ne turpe toral, ne sordida mappa
corruget nares, ne non et cantharus et lanx
ostendat tibi te, ne fidos inter amicos
sit qui dicta foras eliminet, ut coeat par   25
iungaturque pari.   Butram tibi Septiciumque
et nisi cena prior potiorque puella Sabinum
detinet adsumam: locus est et pluribus umbris;
sed nimis arta premunt olidae convivia caprae.
Tu quotus esse velis rescribe et rebus omissis   30
atria servantem postico falle clientem.

VI.

TO NUMICIUS.

Mental sobriety is the secret of happiness. Though free from
the terror of natural phenomena, yet if you are over-anxious
as to wealth or popularity or other personal ambitions you
lose your mental equilibrium.   It is a kind of madness to be
too much enamoured even of virtue itself.

Nil admirari prope res est una, Numici,
solaque, quae possit facere et servare beatum.
Hunc solem et stellas et decedentia certis
tempora momentis sunt qui formidine nulla
imbuti spectent.   Quid censes munera terrae?   5
quid maris extremos Arabas ditantis et Indos?
ludicra quid, plausus et amici dona Quiritis?
quo spectanda modo, quo sensu credis et ore?
qui timet his adversa, fere miratur eodem
quo cupiens pacto; pavor est utrobique molestus,   10
inprovisa simul species externat utrumque.
Gaudeat an doleat, cupiat metuatne, quid ad rem,
si, quidquid vidit melius peiusve sua spe,
defixis oculis animoque et corpore torpet?
insani sapiens nomen ferat, aequus iniqui,   15
ultra quam satis est virtutem si petat ipsam.

Beware then of letting anything destroy your self-control.   There
is nothing lasting; death awaits successful and unsuccessful
alike.

I nunc, argentum et marmor vetus aeraque et artes
suspice, cum gemmis Tyrios mirare colores;
gaude quod spectant oculi te mille loquentem;

navus mane forum et vespertinus pete tectum,   20
ne plus frumenti dotalibus emetat agris
Mutus et (indignum, quod sit peioribus ortus)
hic tibi sit potius quam tu mirabilis illi.
Quidquid sub terrast in apricum proferet aetas ;
defodìet condetque nitentia.   Cum bene notum   25
porticus Agrippae et via te conspexerit Appi,
ire tamen restat, Numa quo devenit et Ancus.

Make up your mind what it is which will bring happiness.
If it is VIRTUE, seek virtue exclusively.

Si latus aut renes morbo temptantur acuto,
quaere fugam morbi.   Vis recte vivere : quis non ?
si virtus hoc una potest dare, fortis omissis   30
hoc age deliciis.

If MONEY, make every exertion and use every prudence to get it.

Virtutem verba putas et
lucum ligna : cave ne portus occupet alter,
ne Cibyratica, ne Bithyna negotia perdas ;
mille talenta rotundentur, totidem altera, porro et
tertia succedant, et quae pars quadret acervum.   35
Scilicet uxorem cum dote fidemque et amicos
et genus et formam regina Pecunia donat,
ac bene nummatum decorat Suadela Venusque.
Mancipiis locuples eget aeris Cappadocum rex :
ne fueris hic tu.   Chlamydes Lucullus, ut aiunt,   40
si posset centum scaenae praebere rogatus,
'qui possum tot ?' ait ; 'tamen et quaeram, et quot habebo
mittam :' post paulo scribit, sibi milia quinque
esse domi chlamydum, partem vel tolleret omnes.
Exilis domus est, ubi non et multa supersunt   45
et dominum fallunt et prosunt furibus.   Ergo

si res sola potest facere et servare beatum,
hoc primus repetas opus, hoc postremus omittas.

If POPULARITY, get a nomenclator and make yourself affable
to all.

Si fortunatum species et gratia praestat,
mercemur servum, qui dictet nomina, laevum   50
qui fodicet latus et cogat trans pondera dextram
porrigere 'hic multum in Fabia valet, ille Velina ;
cui libet hic fasces dabit, eripietque curule
cui volet inportunus ebur.' 'Frater' 'pater' adde ;
ut cuiquest aetas, ita quemque facetus adopta.   55

If GOOD LIVING, go anywhere for a good dinner; never mind
your health ; let the Suitors be your models.

Si bene qui cenat bene vivit, lucet, eamus
quo ducit gula; piscemur, venemur, ut olim
Gargilius, qui mane plagas, venabula, servos,
differtum transire forum populumque iubebat,
unus ut e multis populo spectante referret   60
emptum mulus aprum. Crudi tumidique lavemur,
quid deceat, quid non obliti, Caerite cera
digni, remigium vitiosum Ithacensis Vlixi,
cui potior patria fuit interdicta voluptas.

If LOVE and LAUGHTER, let us love and laugh.

Si, Mimnermus uti censet, sine amore iocisque   65
nil est iucundum, vivas in amore iocisque.

Farewell.

Vive, vale. Siquid novisti rectius istis,
candidus inperti ; si non, his utere mecum.

VII.

TO MAECENAS.

I said I was going into the country for five days, I have been
absent all August. I cannot stand Rome in the dog-days, and
in the winter I mean to go to the sea-coast for retirement and
study.

Quinque dies tibi pollicitus me rure futurum,
Sextilem totum mendax desideror. Atqui
si me vivere vis sanum recteque valentem,
quam mihi das aegro, dabis aegrotare timenti,
Maecenas, veniam, dum ficus prima calorque   5
dissignatorem decorat lictoribus atris,
dum pueris omnis pater et matercula pallet,
officiosaque sedulitas et opella forensis
adducit febres et testamenta resignat.
Quodsi bruma nives Albanis inlinet agris,   10
ad mare descendet vates tuus et sibi parcet
contractusque leget; te, dulcis amice, reviset
cum Zephyris, si concedes, et hirundine prima.

You will excuse me, for your bounty was not from undervaluing
what you gave but because you valued me. A constant
attendance on you would be impossible at my age and with my
feeble health.

Non quo more piris vesci Calaber iubet hospes
tu me fecisti locupletem. 'Vescere, sodes.'   15
'Iam satis est.' 'At tu quantum vis tolle.' 'Benigne.'
'Non invisa feres pueris munuscula parvis.'
'Tam teneor dono, quam si dimittar onustus.'
'Vt libet; haec porcis hodie comedenda relinques.'

Prodigus et stultus donat quae spernit et odit :   20
haec seges ingratos tulit et feret omnibus annis.
Vir bonus et sapiens dignis ait esse paratus,
nec tamen ignorat quid distent aera lupinis.
Dignum praestabo me etiam pro laude merentis :
quodsi me noles usquam discedere, reddes   25
forte latus, nigros angusta fronte capillos,
reddes dulce loqui, reddes ridere decorum, et
inter vina fugam Cinarae maerere protervae.

*If you however take a different view, then I resign all rather
    than give up freedom.   I have always been modest in asking
    favours, see whether I cannot resign them as cheerfully.*

Forte per angustam tenuis volpecula rimam
repserat in cumeram frumenti, pastaque rursus   30
ire foras pleno tendebat corpore frustra ;
cui mustela procul 'si vis' ait 'effugere istinc,
macra cavum repetes artum, quem macra subisti.'
Hac ego si conpellor imagine, cuncta resigno :
nec somnum plebis laudo satur altilium nec   35
otia divitiis Arabum liberrima muto.
Saepe verecundum laudasti, rexque paterque
audisti coram, nec verbo parcius absens :
inspice, si possum donata reponere laetus.

*Your presents on any other terms would be as burdensome as the
    present of horses to Telemachus.*

Haud male Telemachus, proles patientis Vlixi :   40
'non est aptus equis Ithace locus, ut neque planis
porrectus spatiis nec multae prodigus herbae ;
Atride, magis apta tibi tua dona relinquam.'
Parvum parva decent : mihi iam non regia Roma,
sed vacuum Tibur placet aut inbelle Tarentum.   45

To illustrate this take the story of Philippus and the
Auctioneer.

Strenuus et fortis causisque Philippus agendis
clarus, ab officiis octavam circiter horam
dum redit atque foro nimium distare Carinas
iam grandis natu queritur, conspexit, ut aiunt,
adrasum quendam vacua tonsoris in umbra   50
cultello proprios purgantem leniter ungues.
'Demetri,' (puer hic non laeve iussa Philippi
accipiebat) 'abi, quaere et refer, unde domo, quis,
cuius fortunae, quo sit patre quove patrono.'
It, redit et narrat, Volteium nomine Menam,   55
praeconem, tenui censu, sine crimine, notum
et properare loco et cessare, et quaerere et uti,
gaudentem parvisque sodalibus et lare certo
et ludis et post decisa negotia Campo.
'Scitari libet ex ipso quodcumque refers : dic   60
ad cenam veniat.' Non sane credere Mena,
mirari secum tacitus. Quid multa? 'Benigne'
respondet. 'Neget ille mihi?' 'Negat inprobus, et te
neglegit aut horret.' Volteium mane Philippus
vilia vendentem tunicato scruta popello   65
occupat et salvere iubet prior ; ille Philippo
excusare laborem et mercennaria vincla,
quod non mane domum venisset, denique quod non
providisset eum. 'Sic ignovisse putato
me tibi, si cenas hodie mecum.' 'Vt libet.' 'Ergo   70
post nonam venies ; nunc i, rem strenuus auge.'
Vt ventum ad cenamst, dicenda tacenda locutus
tandem dormitum dimittitur. Hic ubi saepe
occultum visus decurrere piscis ad hamum,
mane cliens et iam certus conviva, iubetur   75

rura suburbana indictis comes ire Latinis:
impositus mannis arvum caelumque Sabinum
non cessat laudare. Videt ridetque Philippus,
et sibi dum requiem, dum risus undique quaerit,
dum septem donat sestertia, mutua septem   80
promittit, persuadet uti mercetur agellum.
Mercatur. Ne te longis ambagibus ultra
quam satis est morer: ex nitido fit rusticus atque
sulcos et vineta crepat mera, praeparat ulmos,
inmoritur studiis et amore senescit habendi.   85
Verum ubi oves furto, morbo periere capellae,
spem mentita seges, bos est enectus arando ;
offensus damnis media de nocte caballum
arripit iratusque Philippi tendit ad aedes.
Quem simul adspexit scabrum intonsumque Philippus,   90
'durus' ait, 'Voltei, nimis attentusque videris
esse mihi.' 'Pol, me miserum, patrone, vocares,
si velles' inquit ' verum mihi ponere nomen.
Quod te per Genium dextramque deosque Penates
obsecro et obtestor, vitae me redde priori !'   95

The moral.   Keep to your own station in life.

Qui semel adspexit, quantum dimissa petitis
praestent, mature redeat repetatque relicta.
Metiri se quemque suo modulo ac pede verumst.

VIII.

TO CELSUS.

*Give my compliments to Celsus, Muse, and tell him I am going
on in my old uncertain, restless, and inconsistent way.*

Celso gaudere et bene rem gerere Albinovano
Musa rogata refer, comiti scribaeque Neronis.

Si quaeret quid agam, dic multa et pulchra minantem
vivere nec recte nec suaviter, haud quia grando
contuderit vites oleamve momorderit aestus,   5
nec quia longinquis armentum aegrotet in agris ;
sed quia mente minus validus quam corpore toto
nil audire velim, nil discere, quod levet aegrum ;
fidis offendar medicis, irascar amicis,
cur me funesto properent arcere veterno ;   10
quae nocuere sequar, fugiam quae profore credam ;
Romae Tibur amem ventosus, Tibure Romam.

Then ask after his health, and how he gets on with the Prince,
and tell him not to be spoilt by court favour.

Post haec, ut valeat, quo pacto rem gerat et se,
ut placeat iuveni, percontare, utque cohorti.
Si dicet 'recte,' primum gaudere, subinde   15
praeceptum auriculis hoc instillare memento :
ut tu fortunam, sic nos te, Celse, feremus.

IX.

TO TIBERIUS CLAUDIUS NERO INTRODUCING SEPTIMIUS.

Septimius asks me to introduce him to you, Claudius. I tried to
excuse myself, but in vain. I can honestly say that he is a
man of courage and honour.

Septimius, Claudi, nimirum intellegit unus,
quanti me facias : nam cum rogat et prece cogit,
scilicet ut tibi se laudare et tradere coner,
dignum mente domoque legentis honesta Neronis,
munere cum fungi propioris censet amici ;   5

quid possim videt ac novit me valdius ipso.
Multa quidem dixi, cur excusatus abirem ;
sed timui, mea ne finxisse minora putarer,
dissimulator opis propriae, mihi commodus uni.
Sic ego, maioris fugiens opprobria culpae,   10
frontis ad urbanae descendi praemia.   Quodsi
depositum laudas ob amici iussa pudorem,
scribe tui gregis hunc et fortem crede bonumque.

X.

TO ARISTIUS FUSCUS.

*The only thing about which you and I differ, Fuscus, is that
I love the country, you the town.*

Vrbis amatorem Fuscum salvere iubemus
ruris amatores, hac in re scilicet una
multum dissimiles, at cetera paene gemelli,
fraternis animis quidquid negat alter et alter
adnuimus pariter vetuli notique columbi.   5
Tu nidum servas, ego laudo ruris amoeni
rivos et musco circumlita saxa nemusque.

*Real life and independence can only be got in the country; there
we may 'live according to nature'; and there too all the
physical conditions, warmth and coolness, sweet smells, and
wholesome sleep, are best secured.*

Quid quaeris? Vivo et regno, simul ista reliqui
quae vos ad caelum fertis rumore secundo,
utque sacerdotis fugitivus liba recuso :   10
pane egeo iam mellitis potiore placentis.
Vivere naturae si convenienter oportet,

ponendaeque domo quaerendast area primum:
novistine locum potiorem rure beato?
est ubi plus tepeant hiemes, ubi gratior aura   15
leniat et rabiem Canis et momenta Leonis,
cum semel accepit Solem furibundus acutum?
est ubi divellat somnos minus invida cura?
deterius Libycis olet aut nitet herba lapillis?
purior in vicis aqua tendit rumpere plumbum,   20
quam quae per pronum trepidat cum murmure rivum?

*The attempt to produce a kind of country scene in the town is a
   homage to nature, which is in fact not to be expelled. The
   secret of happiness is to know the true value of things, to
   be content with simple pleasures, and not to be so fond of anything as to be pained at its loss.*

Nempe inter varias nutritur silva columnas,
laudaturque domus, longos quae prospicit agros.
Naturam expelles furca, tamen usque recurret,
et mala perrumpet furtim fastidia victrix.   25
Non qui Sidonio contendere callidus ostro
nescit Aquinatem potantia vellera fucum
certius accipiet damnum propiusve medullis,
quam qui non poterit vero distinguere falsum.
Quem res plus nimio delectavere secundae,   30
mutatae quatient. Siquid mirabere, pones
invitus. Fuge magna: licet sub paupere tecto
reges et regum vita praecurrere amicos.

*This lesson of content illustrated by the story of the horse and
   stag.*

Cervus equum pugna melior communibus herbis
pellebat, donec minor in certamine longo   35
inploravit opes hominis frenumque recepit;
sed postquam victor violens discessit ab hoste,

non equitem dorso, non frenum depulit ore.
Sic qui pauperiem veritus potiore metallis
libertate caret, dominum vehet inprobus atque   40
serviet aeternum, quia parvo nesciet uti.

Discontent like an ill-fitting shoe galls or trips us up.   Reprove
me if I break my own rule, and am too eager for money.

Cui non conveniet sua res, ut calceus olim,
si pede maior erit, subvertet, si minor, uret.
Laetus sorte tua vives sapienter, Aristi,
nec me dimittes incastigatum, ubi plura   45
cogere quam satis est, ac non cessare videbor.
Imperat aut servit collecta pecunia cuique,
tortum digna sequi potius quam ducere funem.

The address.

Haec tibi dictabam post fanum putre Vacunae,
excepto quod non simul esses, cetera laetus.   50

XI.

TO BULLATIUS.

How do you like the cities of Asia, Bullatius?   Do they make
you think meanly of Rome?   Or are you tired of travel and
thinking of settling there?

Quid tibi visa Chios, Bullati, notaque Lesbos,
quid concinna Samos, quid Croesi regia Sardis,
Smyrna quid et Colophon? maiora minorane fama?
cunctane prae Campo et Tiberino flumine sordent,
an venit in votum Attalicis ex urbibus una,   5
an Lebedum laudas odio maris atque viarum?

'Scis, Lebedus quid sit: Gabiis desertior atque
Fidenis vicus; tamen illic vivere vellem,
oblitusque meorum obliviscendus et illis
Neptunum procul e terra spectare furentem.'   10

But after all though an inn is a pleasant refuge in a storm, one
    would not care to live in one. These pleasant places are only
    suitable for a temporary residence: I hope you will soon
    come home and admire them at a distance.

Sed neque, qui Capua Romam petit, imbre lutoque
adspersus volet in caupona vivere; nec qui
frigus collegit, furnos et balnea laudat
ut fortunatam plene praestantia vitam;
nec, si te validus iactaverit Auster in alto,   15
idcirco navem trans Aegaeum mare vendas.
Incolumi Rhodos et Mytilene pulchra facit, quod
paenula solstitio, campestre nivalibus auris,
per brumam Tiberis, Sextili mense caminus.
Dum licet ac voltum servat Fortuna benignum,   20
Romae laudetur Samos et Chios et Rhodos absens.

Still, wherever you are, enjoy the pleasures at hand: reason
    and good sense are the sources of happiness all the world
    over: and we seek by travel what we might find in the
    dullest country town.

Tu quamcumque deus tibi fortunaverit horam
grata sume manu neu dulcia differ in annum,
ut quocumque loco fueris vixisse libenter
te dicas: nam si ratio et prudentia curas,   25
non locus effusi late maris arbiter aufert,
caelum, non animum mutant, qui trans mare currunt.
Strenua nos exercet inertia: navibus atque
quadrigis petimus bene vivere. Quod petis, hic est,
est Vlubris, animus si te non deficit aequus.   30

XII.

TO ICCIUS.

Your position, Iccius, as steward of Agrippa's Sicilian estate is amply sufficient for your wants. Temperance in the midst of luxury turns everything to gold.

Fructibus Agrippae Siculis, quos colligis, Icci,
si recte frueris, non est ut copia maior
ab Iove donari possit tibi. Tolle querellas:
pauper enim non est, cui rerum suppetit usus.
Si ventri bene, si laterist pedibusque tuis, nil   5
divitiae poterunt regales addere maius.
Si forte in medio positorum abstemius herbis
vivis et urtica, sic vives protinus, ut te
confestim liquidus Fortunae rivus inauret,
vel quia naturam mutare pecunia nescit,   10
vel quia cuncta putas una virtute minora.

If in the midst of sordid cares you study the sublime lessons of philosophy is it not as much a subject of admiration as the soul of Democritus soaring away from mundane employments?

Miramur, si Democriti pecus edit agellos
cultaque, dum peregrest animus sine corpore velox,
cum tu inter scabiem tantam et contagia lucri
nil parvum sapias et adhuc sublimia cures: 15
quae mare conpescant causae, quid temperet annum,
stellae sponte sua iussaene vagentur et errent,
quid premat obscurum Lunae, quid proferat orbem,
quid velit et possit rerum concordia discors,
Empedocles an Stertinium deliret acumen?   20

*However, whatever studies you are pursuing, I beg you to receive
Grosphus kindly.*

Verum seu pisces seu porrum et caepe trucidas,
utere Pompeio Grospho et siquid petet ultro
defer : nil Grosphus nisi verum orabit et aequum.
Vilis amicorumst annona, bonis ubi quid deest.

News at Rome.

Ne tamen ignores, quo sit Romana loco res :   25
Cantaber Agrippae, Claudi virtute Neronis
Armenius cecidit ; ius imperiumque Phraates
Caesaris accepit genibus minor ; aurea fruges
Italiae pleno defundit Copia cornu.

XIII.

TO VINIUS ASELLA.

*Deliver the packet to Augustus, Vinius Asina, but only if you
find him in a proper mood.*

Vt proficiscentem docui te saepe diuque,
Augusto reddes signata volumina, Vini,
si validus, si laetus erit, si denique poscet ;
ne studio nostri pecces odiumque libellis
sedulus inportes opera vehemente minister.   5

*If you find it too heavy throw it away rather than tumble and
fall like a true asina. But when you reach Rome don't
make an exhibition of yourself with the parcel, or brag about
having something for Augustus.*

Si te forte meae gravis uret sarcina chartae,
abicito potius, quam quo perferre iuberis

clitellas ferus inpingas, Asinaeque paternum
cognomen vertas in risum et fabula fias.
Viribus uteris per clivos, flumina, lamas;   10
victor propositi simul ac perveneris illuc,
sic positum servabis onus, ne forte sub ala
fasciculum portes librorum ut rusticus agnum,
ut vinosa glomos furtivae Pyrria lanae,
ut cum pilleolo soleas conviva tribulis.   15
Ne volgo narres te sudavisse ferendo
carmina, quae possint oculos auresque morari
Caesaris; oratus multa prece, nitere porro:
vade, vale, cave ne titubes mandataque frangas.

XIV.

TO HIS STEWARD.

*So you don't like the country, Steward!   I on the other hand
grumble at being kept in town by my duty to Lamia.*

Vilice silvarum et mihi me reddentis agelli,
quem tu fastidis, habitatum quinque focis et
quinque bonos solitum Variam dimittere patres,
certemus, spinas animone ego fortius an tu
evellas agro, et melior sit Horatius an res.   5
Me quamvis Lamiae pietas et cura moratur
fratrem maerentis, rapto de fratre dolentis
insolabiliter; tamen istuc mens animusque
fert et amat spatiis obstantia rumpere claustra.

*We envy each other.   Both of us are wrong.   The fault is in
ourselves: we both desire what we have not got.   You com-
plain of the hardships of the country, and miss the luxuries
of town.*

Rure ego viventem, tu dicis in urbe beatum: 10

cui placet alterius, sua nimirumst odio sors.
Stultus uterque locum inmeritum causatur inique :
in culpast animus, qui se non effugit umquam.
Tu mediastinus tacita prece rura petebas,
nunc urbem et ludos et balnea vilicus optas ;   15
me constare mihi scis et discedere tristem,
quandocumque trahunt invisa negotia Romam.
Non eadem miramur : eo disconvenit inter
meque et te : nam quae deserta et inhospita tesqua
credis, amoena vocat mecum qui sentit, et odit   20
quae tu pulchra putas.   Fornix tibi et uncta popina
incutiunt urbis desiderium, video, et quod
angulus iste feret piper et tus ocius uva,
nec vicina subest vinum praebere taberna
quae possit tibi, nec meretrix tibicina, cuius   25
ad strepitum salias terrae gravis : et tamen urgues
iampridem non tacta ligonibus arva, bovemque
disiunctum curas et strictis frondibus exples ;
addit opus pigro rivus, si decidit imber,
multa mole docendus aprico parcere prato.   30

*I on the other hand care nothing for the luxuries of Rome, and
    wish to exchange the envy and detraction that pursue me
    here for the freedom of country life.*

Nunc age, quid nostrum concentum dividat, audi.
Quem tenues decuere togae nitidique capilli,
quem scis inmunem Cinarae placuisse rapaci,
quem bibulum liquidi media de luce Falerni,
cena brevis iuvat et prope rivum somnus in herba :   35
nec lusisse pudet, sed non incidere ludum.
Non istic obliquo oculo mea commoda quisquam
limat, non odio obscuro morsuque venenat ;
rident vicini glaebas et saxa moventem.

You may be sure that the town slave whom you envy, envies you.
It is the old story of the horse and ox. The only golden rule
is 'every one to his trade.'

Cum servis urbana diaria rodere mavis,   40
horum tu in numerum voto ruis; invidet usum
lignorum et pecoris tibi calo argutus et horti.
Optat ephippia bos piger, optat arare caballus;
quam scit uterque, libens, censebo, exerceat artem.

XV.

TO C. NUMONIUS VALA.

Tell me, Vala, the respective advantages of Velia and Salernum;
my doctor forbids Baiae this year. Which of the two has the
best climate, water, bread, game and fish? I want to come back
fat.

Quae sit hiems Veliae, quod caelum, Vala, Salerni,
quorum hominum regio et qualis via (nam mihi Baias
Musa supervacuas Antonius, et tamen illis
me facit invisum, gelida cum perluor unda
per medium frigus. Sane murteta relinqui,   5
dictaque cessantem nervis elidere morbum
sulfura contemni, vicus gemit, invidus aegris
qui caput et stomachum supponere fontibus audent
Clusinis, Gabiosque petunt et frigida rura.
Mutandus locus est et deversoria nota   10
praeteragendus equus. 'Quo tendis? Non mihi Cumas
est iter aut Baias,' laeva stomachosus habena
dicet eques; sed equis frenatost auris in ore;)
maior utrum populum trumenti copia pascat,
collectosne bibant imbres puteosne perennes   15
iugis aquae (nam vina nihil moror illius orae:

rure meo possum quidvis perferre patique ;
ad mare cum veni, generosum et lene requiro,
quod curas abigat, quod cum spe divite manet
in venas animumque meum, quod verba ministret,   20
quod me Lucanae iuvenem commendet amicae ;)
tractus uter plures lepores, uter educet apros ;
utra magis pisces et echinos aequora celent,
pinguis ut inde domum possim Phaeaxque reverti,
scribere te nobis, tibi nos adcredere par est.   25

Such care for good living you think is inconsistent with my pro-
fessions of simplicity and frugality. I am like Maenius,
who first ruined himself with high living and then exclaimed
against spendthrifts.

Maenius, ut rebus maternis atque paternis
fortiter absumptis urbanus coepit haberi,
scurra vagus, non qui certum praesepe teneret,
inpransus non qui civem dinosceret hoste,
quaelibet in quemvis opprobria fingere saevus,   30
pernicies et tempestas barathrumque macelli,
quidquid quaesierat ventri donaret avaro.
Hic, ubi nequitiae fautoribus et timidis nil
aut paullum abstulerat, patinas cenabat omasi
vilis et agninae, tribus ursis quod satis esset,   35
scilicet ut ventres lamna candente nepotum
diceret urendos : correctus Bestius idem,
quidquid erat nactus praedae maioris, ubi omne
verterat in fumum et cinerem, 'non hercule miror,'
aiebat, 'siqui comedunt bona, cum sit obeso   40
nil melius turdo, nil volva pulchrius ampla.'

So I am all for simplicity when my money runs short, for
grandeur when I have a windfall.

Nimirum hic ego sum : nam tuta et parvola laudo,

cum res deficiunt, satis inter vilia fortis :
verum ubi quid melius contingit et unctius, idem
vos sapere et solos aio bene vivere, quorum   45
conspicitur nitidis fundata pecunia villis.

XVI.

TO QUINCTIUS.

To shew you the capabilities of my farm I will describe it.

Ne perconteris, fundus meus, optime Quinti,
arvo pascat erum an bacis opulentet olivae,
pomisne an pratis an amicta vitibus ulmo :
scribetur tibi forma loquaciter et situs agri.
Continui montes, ni dissocientur opaca   5
valle, sed ut veniens dextrum latus adspiciat Sol,
laevum discedens curru fugiente vaporet :
temperiem laudes.   Quid? si rubicunda benigni
corna vepres et pruna ferant, si quercus et ilex
multa fruge pecus, multa dominum iuvet umbra?   10
dicas adductum propius frondere Tarentum.
Fons etiam rivo dare nomen idoneus, ut nec
frigidior Thracam nec purior ambiat Hebrus,
infirmo capiti fluit utilis, utilis alvo.
Hae latebrae dulces et, iam si credis, amoenae,   15
incolumem tibi me praestant Septembribus horis.

*Now as to yourself. All you have to do is to live up to your
    reputation : but beware of three things, (1) don't look for any
    other than self-approval, (2) don't base happiness on anything
    but virtue, (3) don't, as fools to their physician, conceal a
    moral sore because the world calls you sound.*

Tu recte vivis, si curas esse quod audis.

Iactamus iam pridem omnis te Roma beatum ;
sed vereor, necui de te plus quam tibi credas,
neve putes alium sapiente bonoque beatum,   20
neu, si te populus sanum recteque valentem
dictitet, occultam febrem sub tempus edendi
dissimules, donec manibus tremor incidat unctis.
Stultorum incurata pudor malus ulcera celat.

A compliment on victories would not please you if you had
*   never been a soldier; nor should praise for qualities which*
*   you are conscious of not possessing. 'Aye but,' you say, 'no*
*   one can help wishing to be called good!' But remember that*
*   the popular voice can take away as well as give such*
*   reputation.*

Siquis bella tibi terra pugnata marique   25
dicat, et his verbis vacuas permulceat aures :
'Tene magis salvum populus velit, an populum tu,
servet in ambiguo, qui consulit et tibi et urbi,
Iuppiter,' Augusti laudes agnoscere possis ;
cum pateris sapiens emendatusque vocari :   30
respondesne tuo, dic, sodes nomine ? 'Nempe
vir bonus et prudens dici delector ego ac tu.'
Qui dedit hoc hodie, cras si volet auferet, ut si
detulerit fasces indigno, detrahet idem.
'Pone, meumst,' inquit : pono tristisque recedo.   35
Idem si clamet furem, neget esse pudicum,
contendat laqueo collum pressisse paternum :
mordear opprobriis falsis mutemque colores?

Consider what the popular idea of a 'good' man is. Yet such
*   an one may be a hypocrite and inwardly base.*

Falsus honor iuvat et mendax infamia terret
quem nisi mendosum et medicandum ? Vir bonus est quis ?   40
'qui consulta patrum, qui leges iuraque servat,

quo multae magnaeque secantur iudice lites,
quo res sponsore et quo causae teste tenentur.'
Sed videt hunc omnis domus et vicinia tota
introrsum turpem, speciosum pelle decora.   45

Outward compliance with morality brings its own reward, and
*   does not entitle a man to the name of 'good.'   Love of virtue,*
*   not fear of punishment, is the test.   You may judge by trifles*
*   to which no punishment is attached; and by the secret prayers*
*   of the seeming virtuous.*

'Nec furtum feci nec fugi,' si mihi dicat
servus: 'habes pretium, loris non ureris,' aio.
'Non hominem occidi.' 'Non pasces in cruce corvos.'
'Sum bonus et frugi'; renuit negitatque Sabellus.
'Cautus enim metuit foveam lupus accipiterque   50
suspectos laqueos et opertum miluus hamum.
Oderunt peccare boni virtutis amore:
tu nihil admittes in te formidine poenae;
sit spes fallendi, miscebis sacra profanis:
nam de mille fabae modiis cum surripis unum,   55
damnumst, non facinus, mihi pacto lenius isto.'
Vir bonus omne forum quem spectat et omne tribunal,
quandocumque deos vel porco vel bove placat,
'Iane pater' clare, clare cum dixit 'Apollo!'
labra movet metuens audiri 'pulchra Laverna,   60
da mihi fallere, da iusto sanctoque videri,
noctem peccatis et fraudibus obice nubem.'

A man of this sort is a slave, for avarice is slavery.   He may
*   have the benefit of the rule 'don't kill a captive if you can sell*
*   him,'—nothing more.*

Qui melior servo, qui liberior sit avarus,
in triviis fixum cum se demittit ob assem,

non video : nam qui cupiet, metuet quoque ; porro   65
qui metuens vivet, liber mihi non erit umquam.
Perdidit arma, locum virtutis deseruit, qui
semper in augenda festinat et obruitur re.
Vendere cum possis captivum, occidere noli :
serviet utiliter : sine pascat durus aretque,   70
naviget ac mediis hiemet mercator in undis,
annonae prosit, portet frumenta penusque.

The lofty independence of the really good illustrated by the words
of Dionysus in answer to the threats of Pentheus.

Vir bonus et sapiens audebit dicere : ' Pentheu
rector Thebarum, quid me perferre patique
indignum coges?' 'Adimam bona.' ' Nempe pecus, rem,   75
lectos, argentum : tollas licet.'—' In manicis et
compedibus saevo te sub custode tenebo.'
' Ipse deus, simul atque volam, me solvet.' Opinor,
hoc sentit 'moriar.' Mors ultima linea rerumst.

XVII.

TO SCAEVA.

I will give you my ideas as to how one ought to behave in
associations with the great. But first you must make up
your mind whether you would not prefer a life of quiet and
ease.

Quamvis, Scaeva, satis per te tibi consulis et scis,
quo tandem pacto deceat maioribus uti ;
disce, docendus adhuc quae censet amiculus, ut si
caecus iter monstrare velit! tamen aspice, siquid
et nos, quod cures proprium fecisse, loquamur.   5

Si te grata quies et primam somnus in horam
delectat, si te pulvis strepitusque rotarum,
si laedit caupona, Ferentinum ire iubebo :
nam neque divitibus contingunt gaudia solis,
nec vixit male, qui natus moriensque fefellit.   10

If you decide to attempt it, you must take the view of Aristippus
as opposed to that of the Cynic.

Si prodesse tuis paulloque benignius ipsum
te tractare voles, accedes siccus ad unctum.
'Si pranderet olus patienter, regibus uti
nollet Aristippus.' 'Si sciret regibus uti,
fastidiret olus, qui me notat.' Vtrius horum   15
verba probes et facta doce, vel iunior audi,
cur sit Aristippi potior sententia. Namque
mordacem Cynicum sic eludebat, ut aiunt :

The defence of Aristippus.

'Scurror ego ipse mihi, populo tu : rectius hoc et
splendidius multost. Equus ut me portet, alat rex,   20
officium facio ; tu poscis vilia, verum es
dante minor, quamvis fers te nullius egentem.'

I prefer Aristippus, because unlike the Cynic he is ready for
either fortune ; while the Cynic is only comfortable in rags.

Omnis Aristippum decuit color et status et res,
temptantem maiora, fere praesentibus aequum.
Contra quem duplici panno patientia velat,   25
mirabor, vitae via si conversa decebit.
Alter purpureum non exspectabit amictum,
quidlibet indutus celeberrima per loca vadet,
personamque feret non inconcinnus utramque ;
alter Mileti textam cane peius et angui   30
vitabit chlamydem, morietur frigore, si non
rettuleris pannum. Refer et sine vivat ineptus !

There is something after all approaching virtue in pleasing the
great, for it is not in everyone's power, and implies effort and
determination.

Res gerere et captos ostendere civibus hostes,
attingit solium Iovis et caelestia temptat.
Principibus placuisse viris non ultima laus est :   35
non cuivis homini contingit adire Corinthum :
sedit qui timuit, ne non succederet : esto.
Quid? qui pervenit fecitne viriliter? atqui
hic est aut nusquam, quod quaerimus. Hic onus horret,
ut parvis animis et parvo corpore maius;   40
hic subit, et perfert. Aut virtus nomen inanest,
aut decus et pretium recte petit experiens vir.

I don't however recommend persistent asking for favours, for, if
for no other reason, it is less successful than modesty.

Coram rege sua de paupertate tacentes
plus poscente ferent : distat, sumasne pudenter
an rapias; atqui rerum caput hoc erat, hic fons.   45
'Indotata mihi soror est, paupercula mater,
et fundus nec vendibilis nec pascere firmus'
qui dicit, clamat 'victum date.' Succinit alter
'et mihi!' dividuo findetur munere quadra :
sed tacitus pasci si posset corvus, haberet   50
plus dapis, et rixae multo minus invidiaeque.

Constant hints at poverty, made on every occasion of a journey
or the like, soon become disregarded like a beggar's whine.

Brundisium comes aut Surrentum ductus amoenum,
qui queritur salebras et acerbum frigus et imbres,
aut cistam effractam et subducta viatica plorat,
nota refert meretricis acumina, saepe catellam,   55
saepe periscelidem raptam sibi flentis, uti mox

nulla fides damnis verisque doloribus adsit.
Nec semel inrisus triviis attollere curat
fracto crure planum, licet illi plurima manet
lacrima, per sanctum iuratus dicat Osirim :   60
'credite, non ludo ; crudeles tollite claudum.'
'Quaere peregrinum' vicinia rauca reclamat.

XVIII.

TO LOLLIUS.

*Rudeness and personal uncleanliness may masquerade under the
    guise of unconventional liberty; but the right as usual lies
    between the extremes.*

Si bene te novi, metues, līberrime Lolli,
scurrantis speciem praebere, professus amicum.
Vt matrona meretrici dispar erit atque
discolor, infido scurrae distabit amicus.
Est huic diversum vitio vitium prope maius,   5
asperitas agrestis et inconcinna gravisque,
quae se commendat tonsa cute, dentibus atris,
dum vult libertas dici mera veraque virtus.
Virtus est medium vitiorum et utrimque reductum.

One man is too subservient, another too tenacious in trifles.

Alter in obsequium plus aequo pronus et imi   10
derisor lecti sic nutum divitis horret,
sic iterat voces et verba cadentia tollit,
ut puerum saevo credas dictata magistro
reddere, vel partes mimum tractare secundas ;
alter rixatur de lana saepe caprina,   15
propugnat nugis armatus : 'scilicet, ut non

sit mihi prima fides et vere quod placet ut non
acriter elatrem, pretium aetas altera sordet.'
Ambigitur quid enim? Castor sciat an Docilis plus;
Brundisium Minuci melius via ducat an Appi.   20

Rules to be observed in intercourse with the great. (1) *Don't ape
the vices and rival the extravagance of the rich.*

Quem damnosa venus, quem praeceps alea nudat,
gloria quem supra vires et vestit et unguit,
quem tenet argenti sitis inportuna famesque,
quem paupertatis pudor et fuga, dives amicus,
saepe decem vitiis instructior, odit et horret,   25
aut, si non odit, regit ac veluti pia mater
plus quam se sapere et virtutibus esse priorem
volt et ait prope vera: 'meae (contendere noli)
stultitiam patiuntur opes; tibi parvola res est:
arta decet sanum comitem toga; desine mecum   30
certare.' Eutrapelus, cuicumque nocere volebat,
vestimenta dabat pretiosa: beatus enim iam
cum pulchris tunicis sumet nova consilia et spes:
dormiet in lucem, scorto postponet honestum
officium, nummos alienos pascet, ad imum   35
Thraex erit aut olitoris aget mercede caballum.

(2) *Don't pry into your patron's secrets, or blab them.*

Arcanum neque tu scrutaberis illius umquam,
conmissumque teges et vino tortus et ira.

(3) *Don't make too much of your own tastes, and refuse to accom-
pany him hunting, especially as you can excel in it, as you have
done in war,—and indeed you show your tastes by the style of
your amusements at home.*

Nec tua laudabis studia aut aliena reprendes,
nec, cum venari volet ille, poemata panges.   40

Gratia sic fratrum geminorum, Amphionis atque
Zethi, dissiluit, donec suspecta severo
conticuit lyra. Fraternis cessisse putatur
moribus Amphion : tu cede potentis amici
lenibus imperiis, quotiensque educet in agros   45
Aetolis onerata plagis iumenta canesque,
surge et inhumanae senium depone Camenae,
cenes ut pariter pulmenta laboribus empta :
Romanis sollemne viris opus, utile famae
vitaeque et membris, praesertim cum valeas et   50
vel cursu superare canem vel viribus aprum
possis. Adde virilia quod speciosius arma
non est qui tractet : scis, quo clamore coronae
proelia sustineas campestria ; denique saevam
militiam puer et Cantabrica bella tulisti   55
sub duce, qui templis Parthorum signa refigit
nunc et, siquid abest, Italis adiudicat armis.
Ac, ne te retrahas et inexcusabilis absis,
quamvis nil extra numerum fecisse modumque
curas, interdum nugaris rure paterno :   60
partitur lintres exercitus, Actia pugna
te duce per pueros hostili more refertur,
adversarius est frater, lacus Hadria, donec
alterutrum velox victoria fronde coronet.
Consentire suis studiis qui crediderit te,   65
fautor utroque tuum laudabit pollice ludum.

(4) *Don't encourage gossips.*

Protinus ut moneam, siquid monitoris eges tu :
quid de quoque viro et cui dicas, saepe videto.
Percontatorem fugito : nam garrulus idemst,
nec retinent patulae conmissa fideliter aures,   70
et semel emissum volat inrevocabile verbum.

(5) Be careful whom you introduce to your patron. You will
get the discredit of his misconduct.

Qualem commendes, etiam atque etiam aspice, ne mox
incutiant aliena tibi peccata pudorem.
Fallimur, et quondam non dignum tradimus : ergo
quem sua culpa premet, deceptus omitte tueri ;
ut penitus notum, si temptent crimina, serves   80
tuterisque tuo fidentem praesidio : qui
dente Theonino cum circumroditur, ecquid
ad te post paullo ventura pericula sentis ?
nam tua res agitur, paries cum proximus ardet,
et neglecta solent incendia sumere vires.   85

The friendship of the great is not all pleasure, you have to suit
your tastes and moods to his, and to be careful to observe the
mean between dulness and forwardness.

Dulcis inexpertis cultura potentis amici ;
expertus metuit. Tu, dum tua navis in altost,
hoc age, ne mutata retrorsum te ferat aura.
Oderunt hilarem tristes tristemque iocosi,
sedatum celeres, agilem navumque remissi ;   90
potores [bibuli media de nocte Falerni
oderunt] porrecta negantem pocula, quamvis
nocturnos iures te formidare tepores.
Deme supercilio nubem : plerumque modestus
occupat obscuri speciem, taciturnus acerbi.   95

In the midst of all such distractions consult philosophy for the
secret of happiness.

Inter cuncta leges et percontabere doctos,
qua ratione queas traducere leniter aevum,
num te semper inops agitet vexetque cupido,

num pavor et rerum mediocriter utilium spes,
virtutem doctrina paret naturane donet,   100
quid minuat curas, quid te tibi reddat amicum,
quid pure tranquillet, honos an dulce lucellum,
an secretum iter et fallentis semita vitae.

The wise man's prayer.

Me quotiens reficit gelidus Digentia rivus,
quem Mandela bibit, rugosus frigore pagus,   105
quid sentire putas? quid credis, amice, precari?
sit mihi, quod nunc est, etiam minus, et mihi vivam
quod superest aevi, siquid superesse volunt di ;
sit bona librorum et provisae frugis in annum
copia, neu fluitem dubiae spe pendulus horae.   110
Sed satis est orare Iovem, quae donat et aufert :
det vitam, det opes; aequum mi animum ipse parabo.

XIX.

TO MAECENAS.

*I once said, Maecenas, that poetry and water-drinking were
incompatible.*

Prisco si credis, Maecenas docte, Cratino
nulla placere diu nec vivere carmina possunt,
quae scribuntur aquae potoribus. Vt male sanos
adscripsit Liber Satyris Faunisque poetas,
vina fere dulces oluerunt mane Camenae.   5
Laudibus arguitur vini vinosus Homerus ;
Ennius ipse pater numquam nisi potus ad arma
prosiluit dicenda. 'Forum putealque Libonis
mandabo siccis, adimam cantare severis.'

Straightway all our poets took to drinking before noon: as if a
short toga could make a Cato.   Even a casual paleness in me
is imitated.

Hoc simul edixi, non cessavere poetae   10
nocturno certare mero, putere diurno.
Quid? siquis vultu torvo ferus et pede nudo
exiguaeque togae simulet textore Catonem,
virtutemne repraesentet moresque Catonis?
Rupit Iarbitam Timagenis aemula lingua,   15
dum studet urbanus tenditque disertus haberi:
decipit exemplar vitiis imitabile: quod si
pallerem casu, biberent exsangue cuminum.
O imitatores, servum pecus, ut mihi saepe
bilem, saepe iocum vestri movere tumultus !   20

I certainly initiated a new style in Latin poetry, which, though
founded on Greek models, was not a servile imitation of
them.

Libera per vacuum posui vestigia princeps,
non aliena meo pressi pede.   Qui sibi fidit,
dux reget examen.   Parios ego primus iambos
ostendi Latio, numeros animosque secutus
Archilochi, non res et agentia verba Lycamben.   25
Ac ne me foliis ideo brevioribus ornes,
quod timui mutare modos et carminis artem:
temperat Archilochi musam pede mascula Sappho,
temperat Alcaeus, sed rebus et ordine dispar,
nec socerum quaerit, quem versibus oblinat atris,   30
nec sponsae laqueum famoso carmine nectit.
Hunc ego, non alio dictum prius ore, latinus
volgavi fidicen; iuvat inmemorata ferentem
ingenuis oculisque legi manibusque teneri.

Why then am I a favourite in the closet, but unpopular abroad?
   Because I shrink from the publicity of recitations and am
   believed to do so not from modesty but superciliousness.

Scire velis, mea cur ingratus opuscula lector   35
laudet ametque domi, premat extra limen iniquus.
Non ego ventosae plebis suffragia venor
inpensis cenarum et tritae munere vestis;
non ego, nobilium scriptorum auditor et ultor,
grammaticas ambire tribus et pulpita dignor: 40
hinc illae lacrimae. 'Spissis indigna theatris,
scripta pudet recitare et nugis addere pondus'
si dixi, 'rides' ait, 'et Iovis auribus ista
servas: fidis enim, manare poetica mella
te solum, tibi pulcher.' Ad haec ego naribus uti   45
formido et, luctantis acuto ne secer ungui,
'displicet iste locus' clamo et diludia posco.
Ludus enim genuit trepidum certamen et iram,
ira truces inimicitias et funebre bellum.

XX.

TO HIS BOOK.

So you long for publication?   Well go! but you will repent.

Vertumnum Ianumque, liber, spectare videris,
scilicet ut prostes Sosiorum pumice mundus:
odisti claves et grata sigilla pudico;
paucis ostendi gemis et communia laudas,
non ita nutritus. Fuge, quo descendere gestis: 5
non erit emisso reditus tibi. 'Quid miser egi?
quid volui?' dices, ubi quis te laeserit, et scis
in breve te cogi, cum plenus languet amator.

Yet I think you will have your vogue; then you will be con-
signed to the moths, or sent to the provinces, or become a
school-book.

Quod si non odio peccantis desipit augur,
carus eris Romae, donec te deserat aetas ;   10
contrectatus ubi manibus sordescere volgi
coeperis, aut tineas pasces taciturnus inertes,
aut fugies Vticam aut vinctus mitteris Ilerdam.
Ridebit monitor non exauditus, ut ille,
qui male parentem in rupes protrusit asellum   15
iratus : quis enim invitum servare laboret ?
hoc quoque te manet, ut pueros elementa docentem
occupet extremis in vicis balba senectus.

Tell the world your author's history.   Speak me fair; tell them
my birth, habits, and age.

Cum tibi sol tepidus plures admoverit aures,
me libertino natum patre et in tenui re   20
maiores pennas nido extendisse loqueris,
ut quantum generi demas, virtutibus addas ;
me primis urbis belli placuisse domique,
corporis exigui, praecanum, solibus aptum,
irasci celerem, tamen ut placabilis essem.   25
Forte meum siquis te percontabitur aevum :
me quater undenos sciat inplevisse Decembres,
collegam Lepidum quo duxit Lollius anno.

NOTES.

EPISTLE I.

[1—12. Introductory address to Maecenas, for whom see Introduction, § 3, *On the persons addressed in the Epistles.* Maecenas has apparently pressed him to write more Lyrics. He takes the opportunity of stating his views as to the philosophy of life.]

1. *prima...summa* 'You who were the theme of my earliest and shall be of my latest song'. The expression is general and almost proverbial; it must not be wholly referred to the fact that Sat. 1, 1 [much less that Ode 1, 1] begins with the name of Maecenas, nor to any supposed implication that these Epistles are to be the last of the poet's compositions. It simply means to express his great and constant regard for Maecenas, cp. Homer Hymn Ap. 21—3 σὲ δ' ἀοιδὸς...ἡδυεπὴς πρῶτόν τε καὶ ὕστατον αἰὲν ἀείδειν. Vergil Ecl. 8, 11 *a te principium, tibi desinet.*

camena [*Kas* = 'sing', car-men] used by Horace frequently as equivalent to Musa (μοῦσα), even with the epithet *Graecae* (Od. 2, 16, 38): and then as here = 'song', *Paulum...gratus insigni referam Camena* Od. 1, 12, 39. The old form appears to have been *Casmena*, and it is not employed as Horace uses it by the elder poet Lucretius. Vergil (Ecl. 8, 59), Propertius (4, 10, 1), and Ovid (M. 14, 434) use it as equivalent to the Greek *Musa.*

2—3. To ask me to go back to my old style is like taking a gladiator who has served his time, and has been dismissed by the presentation of a wooden sword (*rudis,* cp. Cic. Phil. 2, § 74 *tam bonus gladiator rudem tam cito?*), and placing him again in the gladiatorial barrack (*ludus gladiatorius*). Companies (*familiae*) of gladiators were

kept by magistrates or other rich men for exhibition at the games
(*munera*). They were trained together in barracks, which from being
thus places of instruction were called 'schools' (*ludi*). Sometimes *ludus
gladiatorius* means such a school, sometimes the body of gladiators
themselves.

2. *spectatum satis* 'who has been long enough before the public',
or 'in the arena'.

quaeris includere. This construction of *quaero* and the infinitive is
post-Augustan in prose, but the poets used it : cp. Od. 1, 16, 25 *mutare
quaero.* Ovid Epist. 12, 175 *stultae dum te iactare maritae Quaeris.*

4. *aetas.* Horace, as appears from 20, 28, was in his forty-fifth
year when he published this book, and probably not much more than a
year or two younger when he began it. He was not yet therefore what
was technically called *senex*—or even *senior*: but his *calida iuventus*
was past, and he was conscious of middle age. The usual divisions
of the age of a Roman citizen were 1—17 *puer*, 17—31 *adulescens*
(the age for the quaestorship), 31—46 *iuvenis* (end of military age),
46—61 *senior*, 61—to death *senex.*

Veianius, a well-known gladiator of the day. Porphyrion says that
he consecrated his arms at the temple of Hercules at Fundi, a town on
the coast of Latium (mod. Fondi).

5. *Herculis ad postem.* Just as the sailor who has escaped alive
from shipwreck dedicates his dripping clothes to Neptune (Od. 1, 5,
14), and the writer of love-songs when ceasing that employment
dedicates his lyre to Venus (Od. 3, 26, 3), so the gladiator hangs up his
arms in the temple of Hercules, the god of the games.

abditus 'retired'. Cp. Ter. Hecyr. 174 *senex rus abdidit se: huc
raro in urbem commeat.*

6. *extrema totiens exoret arena* 'that he may not have over and
over again to come to the edge of the arena and beg the people for his
demission', i.e. after some successful contest. This is better than to
explain it, with some, as a reference to the appeal of the conquered
gladiator for mercy (see on 18, 66); for such an appeal would not be
repeated often, nor would it if successful be the end of the gladiator's
service.

7. *est...aurem* 'some one whispers in my ear'. Imitated by Persius
5, 96 *Stat contra ratio et secretam garrit in aurem.*

purgatam, now 'cleansed' from all that would make it deaf to good
advice, such as the passions of youth. The expression had become

proverbial, see Plaut. Mil. 3, 1, 179 *tibi perpurgatis operam dabimus auribus.* Cp. 'The hearts of this people have waxed gross, and their ears are dull of hearing', Is.

8. *sanus* 'if you are wise', εὖ φρονῶν. Horace has probably in his mind the lines of Ennius quoted by Cicero de Sen. § 14

> *Sicut fortis equus, spatio qui saepe supremo*
> *vicit Olympia, nunc senio confectus quiescit.*

Ovid has used the same image, Tr. 4, 8, 19 *Ne cadat et multas palmas inhonestet adeptus, Languidus in pratis gramina carpit equus.*

9. *peccet* 'make a false step', like *titubes* in 13, 19.

ilia ducat 'get broken-winded', lit. 'strain its flanks': so Vergil Georg. 3, 506 *attractus ab alto Spiritus, interdum gemitu gravis, imaque longo Ilia singultu tendunt.*

10—11. I therefore have given up poetry and such trifling and am wholly devoted to philosophy.

quid verum, the obtaining a criterion of truth is properly the object of metaphysics or mental philosophy; but Horace is apparently speaking solely here of ethics and therefore *verum* = 'right', cp. 12, 23. *decens* = honestum [τὸ πρέπον]. Orelli quotes Cicero Off. 1, 27, 94 *et quod decet honestum est, et quod honestum est decet.*

12. That is 'I am laying up a store of wisdom to stand me in stead in my near approaching old-age'. For the metaphor from the storing of wine implied in *condo* and *depromere* cp. Od. 1, 20, 1 *Vile potabis modicis Sabinum Cantharis, Graeca quod ego ipse testa Conditum levi.* Od. 1, 9, 7 *Deprome quadrimum Sabina...merum diota. compono* amplifies *condo*, 'I arrange' 'set in order' for future use: cp. Od. 3, 29, 33 *quod adest memento Componere aequus.* Beware of translating 'compose' in the sense of 'write', though Horace does use the word elsewhere in that sense.

13. *lare* 'household', and so 'school of philosophy': cp. 'the household of faith'. Thus Cicero speaks of the *familia peripateticorum* : cp. also Od. 1, 29, 14 *Socraticam domum.*

14. *addictus* 'bound', a legal word applied to an insolvent debtor handed over by the Praetor to his creditor.

iurare in verba alicuius is to take an oath according to a form of words dictated by another. Thus the soldier was said *iurare in verba*, e.g. *Scipionis*, Livy 28, 29. Hence it comes to mean 'to swear obedience to', as a soldier to his general.

15. *hospes* 'a passing visitor'. Both *magistri* and *deferor* are words used in describing attendance on philosophers. See Cic. Mur. 64.

16. *nunc agilis* etc. i.e. at one time I become a Stoic ; for the Stoics recommended the taking an active part in public affairs ; for, as virtue consists not in contemplation but in action, the wise man must take the opportunity presented by the state of consulting the general benefit, and therefore 'no wise-man can be a private-man', Cic. Tusc. 4, 23, 51. Yet some of the later Stoics thought existing constitutions so bad that they advised their followers to abstain. The practical Roman however did not take this view. *agilis* πρακτικὸς 'practical', 'active', cp. 18, 90—though Horace's political activity was only imaginary.

17. *virtutis*, that is of the ideal virtue which was the *summum bonum* of the Stoics, and consisted in living in conformity with nature.

18. *Aristippi praecepta* 'the doctrines of Aristippus', who was a pupil of Socrates, and who was born at Cyrene about B.C. 430. He does not appear to have left any writings; but the school of philosophers, who more or less adopted the scheme of doctrines attributed to him, were called after his birthplace the 'Cyrenaics'. His versatility in adapting himself to all conditions of life is noticed in 17, 23, where see note. He professed to indulge his passions without being a slave to them, and to be able to find pleasure in whatever position he might be. The opposition of his doctrine to that of the Stoics in regard to the point noticed in the previous line, i.e. in the matter of active participation in political life, is illustrated by an anecdote in Xen. Mem. 2, 1, 13 where he is represented as avowing to Socrates that to avoid all troubles of political life he refused to confine himself to his own city but travelled about a citizen of the world (οὐδ' εἰς πολιτείαν ἐμαυτὸν κατακλείω ἀλλὰ ξένος πανταχοῦ εἰμι). For practical purposes it was the same as Epicureanism.

21. *opus debentibus* 'obliged to labour' all the day; not 'who owe a fixed task', like women with a certain weight of wool; for to such the day would be rather short than long.

22. *pupillis...matrum.* Mothers could not in the legal sense be *tutores* of their children; and were indeed *in tutela* themselves. But no doubt the *tutores* or legal guardians of boys, whose father was dead, placed them in the charge of their mother up to a certain age. Thus the year (the *last* year or more generally the whole period) of pupillage seems slow and long to 'wards' (pupilli) whose mothers are harsh.

27. *restat* refers to the previous lines, 'as circumstances prevent

my getting on as fast as I could wish towards philosophical perfection, I must be content with some elementary improvement'.

28. *non possis* 'though you cannot'. The construction is *non possis contendere quantum Lynceus (contendere potest)*. *Lynceus*, one of the Argonauts, son of Aphareus a Messenian. 'His was the keenest eye of all men upon earth', Pind. Nem. 10, 116. When Castor and Pollux invaded Messenia he saw them, though hidden within an oak.

29. *non tamen* 'yet you are not so hopelessly blind as not to use remedies if you have sore eyes'. That is, though you cannot hope to be perfect you will take second best.

30. *Glyconis*. Glycon, a famous athlete of Pergamum in Asia Minor, is described in the Anthology (7, 692) as 'an irresistible thunderbolt, broad of foot, a new Atlas'.

31. *prohibere*, like other words involving the idea of *separation*, takes the accusative or ablative of either of the things between which the separation is made. Thus the Latins could say *prohibere cheragram corpore* or *corpus cheragra*. See on 8, 10 *me arcere veterno*.

nodosa cheragra. The gout is called *nodosa* from the effect of chalk-stones in the joints, cp. Pers. 5, 57 *cum lapidosa cheragra Fregerit articulos.* See 2, 52.

32. *est quadam tenus* 'a certain way one may go', *quadam (via) tenus*. The preposition *tenus* (originally a subst. = 'stretch') always follows the word it governs, R. 2161. *si* 'although'.

33. *miseroque cupidine* 'the unrest of passion'; *misero* has an active sense, 'that makes miserable', cp. 19, 18. Obs. *cupido* is always masc. in Horace (Or.), cp. *cupidine falso* Sat. 1, 1, 61.

34. *verba et voces.* Certain formulae of philosophy acting like magic incantations (ἐπῳδαί). *vox* is used by Cicero of a philosophical dictum, e.g. de Am. § 59. *dolorem* 'mental disease' as described in v. 33.

37. *ter pure lecto...libello* 'by reading the treatise three times as a mystic purification'. Horace playfully supposes the pious reading of a Stoic treatise to have the same effect as an ordinary rite of purification, such as bathing in clear running water. The mystic value of a treble repetition is often referred to, cp. Pers. 2, 15 *Haec sancte ut poscas, Tiberino gurgite mergis Mane caput bis terque?* Ovid Fast. 41, 313 *ter caput irrorat, ter tollit in aethera palmas.* Cp. also Od. 1, 28, 36 *iniecto ter pulvere curras.*

38. *amator* 'licentious', cp. Od. 3, 4, 79.

41. *virtus est* sc. *prima* 'the first' 'the most elementary virtue':
cp. Quint. 8, 3, 41 *prima virtus est vitio carere.*

43. *censum,* cp. 7, 56. *repulsam* 'rejection' in a candidature for
office.

. 46. *pauperiem fugiens.* Cp. Od. 1, 1, 17 *mox reficit rates Quassas,
indocilis pauperiem pati. per mare, per saxa, per ignes,* sc. in spite
of all difficulties and dangers : cf. Verg. Aen. 2, 527 *per tela per
hostes.*

47. *stulte miraris* 'you regard with unphilosophic desire or
excitement'. Cp. on 6, 1.

48. *meliori,* cp. 2, 68.

49. *circum pagos...pugnax* 'used to engage in the contests at
country festivals' (*paganalia* and *compitalia*). *pugnax* refers to all contests, not merely boxing.

50. *coronari Olympia* 'to win a prize at the Olympic games'.
Olympia is acc. n. pl. 'the Olympic games' and is constructed on the
same analogy as *vincere Olympia* (Cic. de Sen. § 14), νικᾶν 'Ολύμπια.

51. *condicio* 'an offer'. *sine pulvere* 'without trouble': cf.
ἀκονιτί.

53—56. [The next lines are to show how opposite the popular
notions are to this elementary faith of the superiority of virtue.]

54. *Ianus summus ab imo,* that is 'from one end of the forum to
the other'. See 20, 1. The place of business was called *medius Ianus*
(Sat. 2, 3, 18). There were three *Iani* [or square arches pierced with
four entrances] in the forum, *summus, medius* and *imus,* erected in B.C.
174 by the Censors Q. Fulvius Flaccus and A. Postumius Albinus (Liv.
41, 27). It was the place especially used by money-lenders, cp. Ov.
Remed. 561 *Qui Puteal Ianumque timet celeresque kalendas.* And by
this time *medius Ianus* was equivalent to 'the Exchange', Cic. Phil.
6, 5.

55. *prodocet* does not occur elsewhere; Horace seems to have
coined the word in imitation of the Greek προδιδάσκειν, used in similar
sense, e.g. Soph. Aj. 163. Some MSS. have *praedocet* and *perdocet.*

recinunt 'echo each other in saying'. The idea of mutual repetition as well as frequency is included in the verb, cp. *cuius recinet iocosa
Nomen imago* Od. 1, 12, 3 and *Impios parrae recinentis omen Ducat*
Od. 3, 27, 1. Also *cano* and *canto* are used, like our derived word
'cant', to indicate the repetition of commonplaces (τὰ ἀεὶ ὑμνούμενα) as
it were by rote like a lesson set by a master (*dictata*).

56. *suspensi...lacerto.* This line occurs in Sat. 1, 6, 74, describing school-boys with satchel and writing-tablet: it has therefore been some-times supposed to have been foisted in here. It is difficult to see why such an interpolation should have been made: and Horace may very well have intentionally or unintentionally repeated a line which describes the money-lender with his purse and account-book, as well as the school-boy,—just as he has often elsewhere repeated his own lines. For *loculi* as 'purse' or 'money-bag', cp. Juv. 1, 89 *neque enim loculis comitantibus itur Ad casum tabulae posita sed luditur arca.* Cp. Ep. 2, 1, 175. It however seems more often to mean a cabinet of wood or other material for keeping valuables: see the passages quoted by Mayor to the line in Juvenal. For the construction *suspensi loculos lacerto=loculis suspensis lacerto* cp. Verg. Aen. 2, 57 *manus iuvenem post terga revinctum = manibus revinctis.*

58. *quadringentis,* that is to an equestrian fortune, which was 400,000 Sesterces=400 Sestertia, or about £3200. A man who had such a fortune could be enrolled in the *ordo equester,* could wear a gold ring, and sit in a certain part of the theatre [Epode 4, 15], besides being eligible to certain offices.

59. *plebs* 'you will be one of the common people'. The old distinction of plebeian and Patrician had lost its significance; the contrast is now a social one.

59—60. *rex eris,* referring to some game of skill where the best boy is called king. Orelli quotes Suet. Ner. 35 *ducatus et imperia ludere,* 'to play a game of officers and commanders'.

62. *sodes* 'pray' [*si audes,* Cic. Or. 45 § 154 *libenter etiam copulando verba iungebant, ut 'sodes' pro 'si audes', 'sis' pro 'si vis'*]. The uncontracted form occurs in Plaut. Trin. 2, 1, 17 *da mihi hoc, mel meum, si me amas, si audes.*

Roscia lex. The *lex Roscia theatralis* was passed B.C. 68 on the proposition of L. Roscius Otho, in accordance with which fourteen rows of seats behind the orchestra where the Senators sat were reserved for the Equites. Cp. Epode 4, 15. Juv. S. 3, 154—155 *de pulvino surgat equestri Cuius res legi non sufficit.* If a man became bankrupt, or lost property sufficient to bring his fortune below the required amount, he had no more right to occupy the place, cp. Cic. Phil. 2 § 44 *sedisti in quattuordecim ordinibus cum esset lege Roscia decoctoribus certus locus constitutus, quamvis quis fortunae suae vitio non suo decoxisset.* Augustus however relieved all equites from penalties for taking their seat if they or their father had ever possessed the requisite 400,000 Sesterces (Suet. Aug. 14).

nenia 'refrain'. Properly a funeral dirge, it is used for any song, Od. 3, 28, 16 *dicetur merita Nox quoque nenia.* So of a witch's 'incantation', Epode 17, 29 *caputque Marsa dissilire nenia.*

64. *et maribus* 'that was ever on the lips of the manly Curii and Camilli'. Horace uses the plural in general references,—as we say 'your Shakespeares and Miltons', and as Cicero, de Am. § 21, talks of *Paulos, Catones,*—though he is thinking especially of *Manlius Curius Dentatus,* Consul B.C. 290, 275, 274, the conqueror of the Samnites, Sabines, and Pyrrhus, and often mentioned in conjunction with Fabricius [*Caius Fabricius Luscinus,* Cons. 282 and 278] as a type of old-fashioned Roman simplicity. Cp. Od. 1, 12, 41 *incomptum Curium capillis. Camillis,* Lucius Furius Camillus, Cons. B.C. 349, Dictator B.C. 350, 345, the hero of the Gallic wars. This appeal to the simple virtue of the old Roman heroes is paralleled by that of Juvenal in favour of the State Religion, S. 2, 153 *Sed tu vera puta: Curius quid sentit, et ambo Scipiadae? quid Fabricius manesque Camilli?*

decantata, see note on *recinunt* v. 55, and cp. Ter. Hautont. 260 *harum mores cantabat mihi. de* is intensive and iterative, cp. Od. 1, 33, 2 *neu miserabiles decantes elegos.*

67. *ut propius spectes,* i.e. 'that you may sit in seats of the Equites, nearer the stage than those of the common herd', see 1, 62. *Pupi,* we know nothing of this Pupius or his 'whining poems' Horace means,—A mighty privilege! to be in a front seat at the miserable tragedy of Pupius!

68. *responsare* 'to bid defiance to', cp. S. 2, 7, 85 *Responsare cupidinibus, contemnere honores Fortis.*

71. *ut porticibus,* sc. *fruor,* 'as I use the same covered colonnades as they do in my ordinary life in town'. *iudiciis* 'opinions'.

73—5. Your ways, which seem so easy, lead to destruction, and like the fox I learn it by noticing the previous fate of others. The fable is one of Aesop's given by Babrius.

76. *belua multorum es capitum,* that is the people are as various in opinions as in numbers: *quot homines tot sententiae.* Cp. Tennyson, 'After reading a Life and Letters', ''tis but just The *many-headed beast* should know'.

77. *conducere publica* 'to take public contracts', either for collecting taxes, or erecting buildings, or performing other State work, which

were productive of great gains. The contractor was called *redemptor* and was said *redimere* or *conducere* : the State was said *locare.*

78. *frustis* 'slices' or 'helpings' of fish or such dishes : cp. Mart. 11, 27 *frusta cybii.* [It seems impossible to resist the evidence of the MSS. in favour of *frustis* as against *crustis.*] *viduas venentur avaras* 'go hunting for greedy widows', that is, either for marriage or to be put down in their wills. Cp. Mart. 1, 49, 34 *imperia viduarum.* The term *vidua* is applied to any woman without a legal protector, either from having lost a husband, or never having had one, and being deprived of a natural protector as father or brother.

79. *excipiantque senes* : *excipere* is also a hunting term, cp. Od. 3, 12, 12 *excipere aprum.* The hunting of old childish men (*orbi*) by *captatores*, who tried by attentions to get a place in their wills, is often referred to. See the passages quoted by Prof. Mayor to Juvenal 3, 129 ; 4, 19. Cp. Hor. Sat. 2, 5, 28 sq. Notice the subjunctives *venentur* and *excipiant* after the phrase *sunt qui.* With this in prose ' the indicative is unusual unless an adjective of number or definition be added', R. 1681. Horace however uses the indicative, see Od. 1, 1, 4.

quos mittant 'to put into'. Pr. § 150. *vivaria* 'fish ponds' or 'stews'. The keeping of magnificent fish ponds had become a prevalent fashion among the Roman wealthy classes. Cicero speaks with contempt of the frivolity of the *piscinarii*, who cared for nothing in the State as long as 'they had bearded mullets in their fish ponds which would come to their hands', ad Att. 1, 19, 6 ; 2, 1, 7. See also the passages quoted by Mayor to Juv. 4, 51, and Becker's *Gallus*, p. 460.

80. *occulto* 'hidden', because the interest exacted was probably above the legal rate of 12 p. c. See Sat. 1, 2, 14, where five times that amount is mentioned. For various enactments controlling the rate of interest see Ramsay, *Roman Antiquities*, p. 420.

83. *Bais*, Baiae on the Bay of Naples, five miles South of Cumae, and three North of Puteoli. ' The extraordinary mildness of the climate made it an agreeable place of sojourn even in winter, and there was no season of the year when the trees did not present fruits, and the gardens flowers'. It was also a health resort from its hot sulphur-baths, Mart. 64, 3. See Becker's *Gallus*, p. 85 sq. *amoenis* 'lovely', from the root *am-*, as in amo. Cp. 14, 20.

84. *lacus*, sc. Lucrinus. The lake and sea feel the passion of the master, because he builds his villa into them. Cp. Od. 2, 18, 20

*Marisque Baiis obstrepentis urges Summovere litora, Parum locuples
continente ripa.* Cp. Od. 2, 15, 1.

85. *libido* 'caprice'.

86. *fecerit auspicium* 'give the word', 'act as his inspiration'. Or.
well quotes Verg. Aen. 9, 185 *an sua cuique deus fit dira cupido.*

87. *lectus genialis in aulast.* On the marriage of the master of
the house a symbolical marriage-bed was spread in the *atrium* opposite
the door, whence it was sometimes called the *lectus adversus.* Becker's
Gallus, p. 247.

89. *maritis* 'married men'.

90. *teneam* 'am I to hold?' for the subj. in rhetorical or dubitative questions see R. § 1610.

Protea, declined as a Greek word Πρωτεύς, R. 482. The god of the
sea: for his transformations see Verg. G. 4, 440

> *Ille suae non immemor artis
> omnia transformat sese in miracula rerum,
> ignemque, horribilemque feram, fluviumque liquentem.*

91. *cenacula* 'garrets', the upper stories of houses let out as lodgings
and often approached by outside staircases.

92. *balnea,* the cheap baths at which the poorer sort bathed at the
charge of a *quadrans,* Juv. 2, 152. A little after this time public baths
free of charge were left by Agrippa and others, or established by the
various Emperors.

93. *priva triremis* 'a private yacht': the word *triremis* is used
loosely for any large vessel, and the exact sense of 'trireme' must not
be pressed. Cp. Od. 3, 1, 39 *neque (cura) decedit aerata triremi.*

94. *inaequali tonsore* 'a barber who cuts one side shorter than the
other'. This is one of those ablatives which look like an ablative of
agent without *ab.* It may perhaps be explained by regarding *ineq. tons.*
as abl. of circumstance = 'with a bungler for my barber'.

95—6. *subucula...tunicae* 'if by chance I have a worn shabby shirt
under a new tunic with long nap'. *pexa,* from *pecto* 'to comb', means
'with long nap'; thus *toga pexa* 'a new toga', Mart. 2, 44, 1, and a long
beard is called *barba pexa* Mart. 7, 51. The *tunica superior* was a close-
fitting garment worn outside in the house or under the toga abroad.
The *subucula* or *tunica interior* was a shirt.

96. *si toga dissidet impar* 'if my toga is badly arranged and hangs
down more one side than the other'. For the mode of adjusting

the *toga*, see Becker's *Gallus*, p. 411 sq. Cp. Sat. 1, 3, 31 *toga defluit.*

99. *aestuat* 'is restless as the sea'. *disconvenit* 'is inconsistent'.

101. *sollemnia* 'in the ordinary way': an adjective taking the place of an interior or cognate accusative after *insanire*, expressing the extent of action, cp. *acerba tuens* Verg. Aen. 9, 794. R. 1094.

102. *curatoris a praetore dati.* The curator was assigned to a youth between 15 and 25, if necessary to protect his interests; or to a man later on, who was either *furiosus*, or so recklessly extravagant as to appear unfit to manage his property. See Cic. de Sen. § 22 *male rem gerentibus patribus bonis interdici solet.* Cp. Sat. 2, 3, 218 *ad sanos abeat tutela propinquos.*

104. *cum sis* 'though you are'. *tutela* = tutor, but not in the legal sense, only as equivalent to protector, cp. Od. 1, 1, 2 *Maecenas—Oh et praesidium et dulce decus meum.*

105. *te respicientis* 'looking to you for protection and guidance'. A. P. 317 *Respicere exemplar vitae morumque iubebo Doctum imitatorem et veras hinc ducere voces.*

106. He sums up with the famous Stoic paradox that the Wise Man has every perfection, and is able to do everything. Cp. Sat. 2, 2. 'The wise man only is free, because he alone uses his own will and controls himself; alone beautiful, because only virtue is beautiful and attractive; alone rich and happy, because goods of the soul are the most valuable, and true riches consist in being independent of wants... The wise only know how to obey, and they also only know how to govern; they only are therefore kings generals and pilots'. Zeller, *Stoics and Epicureans*, p. 253.

108. *praecipue* 'above all'. *sanus* refers to both mind and body, though Horace turns it, by suddenly introducing the exception of a cold in the head (an illustration drawn from Stoic writers also), to a reference to bodily soundness.

EPISTLE II.

[Written while on a visit to a friend at Praeneste to Lollius Maximus who is staying at Rome for his legal business.]

1. *Lolli.* See Introduction, § 3 and Ep. 13. For the inversion of the names *Lollius Maximus* see on 15, 3.

2. *Praeneste*, a Latin town twenty-seven miles from Rome, mod. *Palestrina.* It was a favourite summer resort of Augustus and his successors and many of the Roman nobles, and is reckoned among other pleasant places of residence by Horace as the 'cool Praeneste', Od. 3, 4, 23.

4. *Chrysippo et Crantore*, two philosophers, the one a Stoic, the other an Academician.

Chrysippus, born B.C. 280 at Soli in Cilicia, succeded Cleanthes as president of the Stoic School.

Crantor, born circ. B.C. 350, also at Soli in Cilicia, was a pupil of Xenocrates at Athens, the head of the Academy. He left a large number of moral works some of which were well known at Rome, especially a treatise *de Luctu.*

7. *barbariae*, here = 'Troy', it is any country non-Greek. *duello* 'war'. [The word *duellum* = 'an engagement between two' is an old form of *bellum*, cp. *du-o* and *bis* for the change *d* into *b*. Thus the Greek form of the name Duilius is Βίλιος.] *lento* 'lingering'.

8. *aestus* 'stormy and changeful passions', cf. *aestuat* 1, 99.

9. *Antenor.* See Il. 7, 348

> 'Give ear, ye Trojans, Dardans, and allies
> While I shall utter all my heart commands.
> Up! let us lead the Argive queen away
> With all her dower, and to the sons of Atreus
> Restore her: stained with perjury we fight
> And therefore all in vain'.

10. *quid Paris*, sc. *respondet*? See ib. l. 362

> 'The woman will I not restore; the wealth
> I brought from Argos to my home with her,—
> That will I give and more will I add thereto'.

11. *Nestor.* See his speech Il. 1, 254—284.

12. *inter...inter.* Or. quotes Cic. de Am. § 95 *quid intersit inter popularem, id est, assentatorem et levem civem, et inter constantem, severum, et gravem.* Cp. 4, 12.

14. The Greek host are punished by the pestilence, and the inroads of Hector while Achilles sulked.

18. *Ulixen.* Horace seems to be thinking of Ulysses as the hero of the Odyssey, not as the wise counsellor and cunning warrior in

the Iliad: the opening lines of the former are still more closely translated in the A. P. 141—2.

22. *inmersabilis* 'not to be drowned' or 'overpowered', cp. Od. 4, 4, 65 *merses profundo ; pulchrior evenit.*

adversis rerum undis 'a sea of troubles '.

23. *Sirenum...Circae.* Odyss. 12, 39 sq.; 10, 230 sq.; and see below 6, 63.

25. *turpis et excors* 'lost to human shape and reason', i.e. an ugly and irrational swine.

27. *nos* 'we ordinary people'. Without going so far as the crew of Ulysses, we idlers in general have the vulgar foibles of the worthless suitors. *sponsi* used irregularly for *proci.*

numerus 'a mere crowd of ciphers', without special qualities. *fruges consumere nati.* Il. 6, 142 οἳ ἀρούρης καρπὸν ἔδουσιν. For constr. cp. 64; R. 1363.

28—29. *Alcinoi...iuventus,* Alcinous king of the Phaeacians [see 15, 24] tells Ulysses his guest (Odyss. 8. 248)

> 'Ever we love sweet feast, and harp, and dance,
> Changes of robes, warm baths, and couches soft '.

31. *cessatum ducere* 'to bring care to cease'. Cp. Od. 4, 11, 35 *minuentur atrae Carmine curae.* And for the supine Sat. 2, 4, 89 *Ducere me auditum.*

32. Horace leaves Homer to begin a declamation suggested by the last two examples against procrastination in moral reform and listlessness.

de nocte 'before day-break'. So *de die,* 'before nightfall', Liv. 23, 8. Cp. *in comitium Milo de nocte venit : Metellus cum prima luce in campum currebat,* Cic. Att. 4, 3. Cp. 14, 34.

34. *curres hydropicus* 'you will have (by your doctor's orders) to run when you are dropsical'. Frequent walking and even running was ordered by the doctors for such patients.

ni,=nisi or *si non,* takes indic. in direct speech, cp. Aen. 1, 392 *Ni frustra augurium vani docuere parentes,* with ib. 2, 178 *Canit Chalcas ...omina ni repetant Argis numenque reducant.*

37. *vigil* ' unable to sleep '.

39. *est animum* 'saps the soul'. Cp. Verg. Aen. 12, 801 *nec te tantus edat tacitam dolor. curandi* sc. *animum. in annum,* 'year after year ', cp. 11, 23 ; 18, 109.

40. *dimidium* 'well begun is half done ', ἀρχὴ δέ τοι ἥμισυ παντός.

42. *rusticus exspectat* 'is like a rustic waiting'. In such comparisons *ut* or some similar word is often omitted, see 3, 34; 15, 34.

dum defluat 'until it shall flow past', with this sense *dum* requires subjunctive. R. 1664.

44. *beata* 'rich', cp. Od. 3, 73 *Thyna merce beatum.* Od. 3, 29, 11 *beatae Romae. pueris creandis* 'for the sake of having children'. The dative with gerundive (which might equally be genitive) expresses work contemplated. Cp. such phrases as *comitia censoribus creandis habuit. Decemviri legibus scribendis.* R. 1156.

45. *pacantur* 'are reduced to cultivation from a state of wildness', a harsh use of *pacare*, similar instances being only quoted from the poets of the silver age. Cp. the phrase *mitiget ferro agrum* Ep. 2, 2, 186. In Verg. Aen. 6, 803 *nemora Erymanthi pacarit* refers entirely to the destruction of the boar. Cp. Aesch. Eum. 13 κελευθοποιοὶ παῖδες Ἡφαίστου χθόνα ἀνήμερον τιθέντες ἡμερωμένην.

47. *domus* 'town house', Od. 2, 3, 18 *cedes coemptis saltibus, et domo, Villaque flavus quam Tiberis lavit. fundus* 'landed property' with farm-house or villa, Od. 1, 12, 43 *avitus apto cum Lare fundus.*

49. *valeat oportet*, obs. omission of *ut*, Pr. p. 149.

50. *conportatis* 'collected and housed'. It is a word used especially of *corn*. See Caes. B. C. 3, 42: Cic. Att. 5, 18. Also of other goods, Cic. de Or. 3 § 92 *nobis opus est rebus exquisitis, undique collectis, arcessitis, comportatis. bene* 'to his own comfort'. Cp. Od. 2, 16, 13 *Vivitur parvo bene.*

51—2. *sic—ut* 'no more than'. Cp. *Ut vivam Maenius? aut sic Ut Nomentanus?* 'no better than Nomentanus' Sat. 1, 1, 101. Fair possessions only add irritation to sickness as pictures irritate sore eyes, fomentations the pain of the gout which they are meant to cure, and the sound of music aching ears.

52. *lippus* 1, 29. *podagram*, cf. *cheragra* 1, 31. Both mean gout, the former in the feet, the latter in the hands. Cp. Mart. 1, 98

> *Litigat et podagra Diodorus, Flacce, laborat:*
> *Sed nil patrono porrigit: haec cheragra est.*

> 'Gouty? But, see, all day in court he stands.
> And pays? Ah no: the gout is in his hands'.

54. *sincerum* 'clean' [R. sim-, cp. simplex], cp. v. 69.

56. *certum finem*, cp. S. 1, 1, 92 *Denique sit finis quaerendi.*

58. *Siculi tyranni.* The cruelty of the Sicilian tyrants Phalaris

(Agrigentum), Agathocles, and the two Dionysii (Syracuse), had made the *Sicula aula* (Juv. 6, 486) proverbial. Cp. Od. 3, 1, 18 (the sword of Damocles). Pers. 3, 39 *Anne magis Siculi gemuerunt aera iuvenci, Et magis auratis pendens laquearibus ensis?* The cruelties of Phalaris seem well supported, see Prof. Mayor's note on Juv. 8, 81 : those of the two Dionysii rest on later writers such as Cicero, Diodorus and Plutarch ; while the accusations against Agathocles are contradicted by much that is known of him.

60. *mens* 'impulse', 'anger'. Cp. Od. 1, 16, 22 *Compesce mentem. dolor* 'the sting of wrath'. Cp. Epode 15, 16 *Si certus intrarit dolor.* Verg. Aen. 48 *quo numine laeso? Quidve dolens regina deum* etc.

61. *poenas festinat* 'eagerly seeks vengeance'. This transitive use of *festinare* is prae-classical, and again of the silver age. The edd. quote the parallel use of *propero* (3, 28) and *depropero* (Od. 3, 24, 61 ; 2, 7, 24). *odio inulto.* Some Editors take this as the dative depending on *poenas festinat,* 'for his insatiate wrath'. But the genitive would be the right construction, see Cic. Att. 1, 16, 7 *putaverunt...fore ut aperte victrix nequitia et libido poenas ab optimo quoque peteret sui doloris.* Nor do I think a parallel instance of the dat. construction can be found. I take it as a descriptive ablative, 'with unchecked bitterness'. For the meaning of *inulto* cp. Od. 1, 2, 51 *Neu sinas Medos equitare inultos.*

62. *ira furor brevis est,* ὀργὴ μανία ὀλιγοχρόνιος, 'anger is madness, only differing from ordinary madness in being transient'. All antirational emotions are foreign to the 'wise man' of the Stoics. Anger especially, as Seneca shows, has all the external marks of madness, 'the expression is bold and threatening, the brow lowering, the face fierce, the step quickened, the hands restless, the colour changed, the breath drawn frequently and rapidly'. Sen. de Ira 1, 1, 3.

63. *tu.* Often used in maxims. Cp. Od. 1, 7, 17 *sic tu sapiens finire memento Tristitiam...Molli mero*: 1, 9, 16 *nec dulces amores Sperne puer, neque tu choreas.* See also Verg. Georg. 5, 73 ; 4, 62.

64. *fingit ire* 'teaches it to go'. *fingere* 'to form by instruction'. *voce paterna Fingeris ad rectum,* A. P. 367; Od. 3, 6, 22 *fingitur artibus:* hence Hor. uses it here as = *docet.*

65. *qua monstret eques* 'in which the rider shows him (by guiding) that he is to go'. Edd. quote Verg. Aen. 1, 418 *Corripuere viam interea qua semita monstrat.* See also Ov. Met. 4, 437 *Qua sit iter,*

manes, Stygiam qua ducat ad urbem, Ignorant. [Most MSS. have *quam.*] For the early training of a horse see Verg. Georg. 3, 190 sq.

66. *cervinam.* A stuffed stag's skin set up in the court-yard to train the hounds. The *aula* here is an outer court, for cattle etc., cp. Propert. 4, 12, 39 *pastoris in aulam. latravit*, trans. 'barked at'. Cp. Sat. 2, 1, 85. Cp. Shak. 'I'd rather be a dog and *bay* the moon'.

68. *verba*, cp. 1, 34. *nunc*, i.e., while you are young. *te melioribus offer*, cp. 1, 48.

69. *recens* 'when it was new'.

70. *anteis* 'go too fast (in reform) for me', cp. 6, 16.

EPISTLE III.

[In the year B.C. 20 Augustus sent his stepson and successor, Tiberius Claudius Nero, to Armenia to depose Artabazus, and on the petition of the Armenians to restore Tigranes his brother, who was at Rome, to the throne. Dio 50, 9. Tiberius had an army and a commission for settling other parts in the East, Paterc. 2, 94; and of course was accompanied by a staff of legati and other officers, one of whom was Julius Florus to whom this letter is written.]

2. *privignus* 'stepson' [*privi-genus* 'of a separate race']. Tiberius was the son of Tiberius Nero and Livia, whom Augustus married, after forcing her husband to divorce her. Tiberius was now 22 years old.

3. Thraca (sometimes Thrace), Θράκη = Θρηικίη, through which Tiberius led his army into the East, after passing through Macedonia (Suet. Tib. 14). In Roman times Thrace was the district North of the Propontis, bounded on the East by the Black Sea, Bulgaria, E. Roumelia and Turkey. Though the winter is severe sometimes in this district, it is by no means so cold as the poets Vergil, Horace, and Ovid represent.

Hebrus, mod. *Maritza*. Its coldness is often referred to in the poets, see 16, 13. Verg. Aen. 12, 331 *gelidi flumina Hebri*. Not that the water was colder than other water, but it was in the North, the land of cold, and was at times frozen over (*nivali compede*) : cp. Od. 3, 25, 10 *Hebrum prospiciens et nive candidam Thracen.*

4. *freta*, The Dardanelles. *vicinas turres*, i.e. of Sestos and Abydos, where the strait is about a mile across, and where, according to Porphyrion, two towers called Hero and Leander, after the hero and heroine of the well-known tale, stood opposite to each other.

5. *Asiae*, what we should call Asia Minor. Claudius' primary commission was to Armenia, a district extending from the Caucasus to the head of the Persian Gulf, and including the mod. Georgia and parts of Turkey in Asia, and Persia. The *pingues campi* refer to the rich grassy plains in this district famous for their breed of horses.

6. *cohors*, the technical term for the officials making up the staff of a commander or provincial governor. For instances see Cic. Verr. 2, § 66 : Ep. ad Q. F. 1, 1, § 12.

quid operum ' what compositions?' so *opuscula* 4, 3; 19, 35.

7. *bella et paces* 'wars and glorious peace secured for the world'. Though some would translate ' the wars of Augustus and his administration in peace'. But the reference seems more general to the glorious result of his wars in forcing all the world to keep the peace. The achievements of Augustus in this respect are often noted by Horace. See Od. 1, 12, 52—5, 2, 9, 19—24; 3, 8, 18—24; 14, 13; 4, 14. The prevailing idea in all these passages is that the arms of Augustus have secured peace all over the Roman world.

longum diffundit in aevum 'transmits (in writing) to distant posterity'. Horace probably means that these achievements of Augustus are to form the theme of a poem, which shall prevent the memory of them dying for want of a *pius vates* (Od. 4, 9, 27—33). For the sense of *aevum* 'a life of fame', cp. Od. 2, 2, 4 *Vivet extento Proculeius aevo.*

9. *Titius.* This Titius is called by the Scholiast (published by Cruquius) 'Titius Septimius a writer of Lyrics and tragedies in the time of Augustus', and has been identified by some with the Septimius of Od. 2, 6, and with Septimius whom Horace introduces to Claudius in Epist. 9 of this book. There are however good reasons for doubting this identification. The Titius here mentioned is evidently junior to Horace, and all we need know of him is that he had been attempting to translate or imitate the odes of Pindar in Latin. Horace playfully hints at the difficulty or hopelessness of the task, which he elsewhere enforces, see Od. 4, 2.

venturus in ora ' destined soon to be the talk of Rome', cf. Ennius, *volito vivus per ora virum.* Propert. 4, 9, 32 *venies tu quoque in ora virum.*

10. *expalluit haustus* 'turned pale at ', 'feared ': cp. Od. 3, 27, 27 *mediasque fraudes palluit audax.* Pers. 1, 124 *Iratum Eupolidem praegrandi cum sene palles.* 5, 183 *sabbata palles.* Cp. the construction of *horreo, festinare* (2, 60), and many other intransitive verbs

used transitively by a stretch of conception, for a list of which see R. § 1123.

11. *lacus...rivos apertos*, that is, 'the common themes and style of poetry'. Cp. Lucr. 4, 2 *iuvat integros accedere fontes Atque haurire.* Hor. Sat. 2, 4, 93 *mihi cura Non mediocris inest fontes ut adire remotos Atque haurire queam vitae praecepta beatae.*

12. *fidibus Latinis* 'Latin lyric poetry'. Ep. 2, 2, 143 *verba sequi fidibus modulanda Latinis.* A. P. 82 *Musa dedit fidibus divos puerosque deorum...referre.* Horace calls himself *Romanae fidicen lyrae* Od. 4, 3, 22, and says that he was *Princeps Aeolium carmen ad Italos Deduxisse modos* (Od. 3, 30, 13), cp. 19, 24 sq.; and there is some sense of his particular province being invaded by Titius. *Thebanos modos* 'the poems of Pindar' (b. about B.C. 520 at Thebes or in its territory).

14. *desaevit* 'rages': cp. the use of *saevit* of a swollen river, Od. 4, 14, 27. The *de-* is intensive as in such words as *defatigare, demereor, deperire,* see R. 1918.

ampullatur 'uses high-flown language'. Horace seems to have coined this word to translate the Greek ληκυθίζειν, 'to magnify common things', 'to speak bombastically'. *ampulla* (amb-olla) 'a round vessel with two handles', λήκυθος. Cp. A. P. 97 *Proiicit ampullas et sesquipedalia verba.* [Prof. Wilkins explains it with reference to the use of the *ampulla* for holding pigments 'dashes on his colours'. I think this difficult to reconcile with the line in A. P.; *ampullor* seems coined like *scurror* from *scurra.*]

15. *quid mihi Celsus agit?* 'How is my Celsus getting on?' *quid agis?* is an ordinary phrase of greeting, cp. Sat. 1, 9, 4 *quid agis, dulcissime rerum?* Another exactly answering also to our 'How d'ye do?' was *ut vales?* [Terence Haut. 406]. Used in this way they do not expect an answer; but the phrase used in a letter is more decidedly a question expecting some answer. For *mihi, ethic dative,* see Pr. § 107.

For *Celsus* see on 8, 1.

15—17. Whom I have often warned, and shall have to do so again, to be original and not use old books too freely.

Palatinus Apollo. The temple of Apollo, built by Augustus on the Palatine after the battle of Actium and dedicated in B.C. 28, had many large buildings attached to it, among them a celebrated library,— *porticus cum bibliotheca Latina Graecaque* [Suet. Aug. 29]. Ovid gives a description of it [Trist. 3, 1, 59],

Inde tenore pari gradibus sublimia celsis,
  Ducor ad intonsi candida templa dei.
Signa peregrinis ubi sunt alterna columnis,
  Belides et stricto barbarus ense pater.
Quaeque viri docto veteres coepere novique
  pectore, lecturis inspicienda patent.

19—20. *cornicula—coloribus.* In the fable as translated from
Aesop by Phaedrus [1, 3] the bird that steals the feathers is a jackdaw
(*graculus*). *cornicula* 'a crow' is a contemptuous diminutive of *cornix,*
and does appear to be used elsewhere.

ipse quid audes? 'what literary composition are you venturing upon
yourself?' Cp. Sat. 2, 1, 10 *Aut si tantus amor scribendi te rapit, aude
Caesaris invicti res dicere.* At the same time it must be remembered
that *audes* is used in a milder and more conventional sense than 'to be
bold enough': see on 1, 62 *sodes.*

22. *turpiter hirtum* 'disgracing you by its uncouthness'. Cp.
A. P. 3 *turpiter atrum. hirtus* is properly 'hairy', 'rough'. As
applied to character it is almost entirely post-Augustan. Cp. Velleius 2,
11 *L. Marius natus equestri loco, hirtus atque horridus, vitaque sanctus.*

23—24. *causis*, as patronus in law-suits: *Insigne maestis praesidium
reis* Od. 2, 1, 13. *civica iura respondere,* 'to give opinions on dis-
puted points of law' was the profession of the *iuris consulti* or *iuris pru-
dentes. iura civica* 'the law of the land' as opposed to *ius gentium.*

carmen amabile should mean 'a delightful song', but perhaps by a
stretch of the meaning of the adjective it may mean 'love ditty', as in
Od. 4, 3, 14 *inter amabiles Vatum choros* may mean 'in the ranks of
the poets of love'.

25. *hederae,* used especially of the crown of a poet, cp. Od. 1, 1, 29
Me doctarum hederae praemia frontium Dis miscent superis.

26. *frigida curarum fomenta* 'those vain remedies of anxiety',
θαλπτήρια ψυχρὰ μεριμνῶν. Thus Ovid in his distress calls the Muses
solacia frigida (Pont. 1, 2, 45); and Plin. Ep. 1, 9 *quot dies quam
frigidis rebus absumpsi.* The 'vain remedies' meant here are the
pursuit of business and gain. Orelli takes *frigida* actively, 'chilling
noble impulses'. Others have taken *fomenta* like *irritamenta* 'that
nourish and produce care'. Horace however uses the word always as
= alleviation, see 2, 52; Epod. 11, 17; Sat. 1, 1, 82. So Plin. Ep.
4, 21; 6, 7 uses it for 'consolation'.

28. *properemus, active,* cp. 2, 61.

29. If we wish to be good citizens and have a good conscience. Cp. 18, 101.

30. *curae, dative*, see Pr. § 108.

31. *Munatius.* We know nothing of this man or of his cause of quarrel with Julius Florus. There is a L. Munatius Plancus to whom Od. 1, 7 is addressed, who was a correspondent of Cicero, and Consul B.C. 42 [Od. 3, 14, 27]. This may be his son.

34. *indomita cervice feros* 'like wild horses unbroken', cp. 2, 64. Od. 2, 5, 1 *Nondum subacta ferre iugum valet Cervice.* For omission of *ut* see 2, 41.

35. *indigni rumpere* 'too good to break'. The prose construction of *dignus* and *indignus* is with *qui* and subj.; but Horace uses them with infinitive, cp. Sat. 1, 3, 24 *Stultus et improbus hic amor est dignusque notari*, where see Palmer's note.

fraternum foedus, cp. 10, 4.

36. A young heifer is fattening for a thank-offering, vowed for the return of you both [*vestrum* not *tuum*]. When Horace offered a thank-offering for his own safety he could afford nothing but a lamb. Od. 2, 17, 32. His friend's return is a greater occasion, as is that of his friend Numida. Cp. Od. 1, 36, 1 *Et ture et fidibus iuvat Placare et vituli sanguine debito Custodes Numidae deos.*

EPISTLE IV.

1. *Albi*, for the poet Albius Tibullus, see Introduction § 3.

candide 'honest and yet friendly'. Horace is fond of applying this epithet to his friends, e.g. to Maecenas Epod. 14, 5; to Furnius, Sat. 1, 10, 86. And Vergil, Plotius, and Varius are *animae, quales neque candidiores Terra tulit, neque queis me sit devinctior alter.* Orelli also quotes Martial 4, 87, 4 *Nil exactius eruditiusquest, Sed nec candidius benigniusque.* By *sermonum* he means his Satires.

2. *regione Pedana.* Pedum is probably the modern Gallicano between Tivoli (Tibur) and Palaestrina (Praeneste) and about 18 miles from Rome. It stood on a hill between two torrents which nearly encircled it. The neighbourhood was a favourite summer resort of the Romans.

3. *quod vincat* 'a poem to surpass'. Pr. § 150: but it is also a dependent sentence, and as such would have the subj. Cp. 13, 17.

Cassi Parmensis. The identity of Cassius of Parma has been a sub-

ject of much controversy : some believing that he is the same poet as
the rapid writer ridiculed in Sat. 1, 10, 62, who however seems cer-
tainly to have been a different person. Cassius of Parma is probably
the Lucius Cassius, whose letter to Cicero is preserved in the Cicero
correspondence (Fam. 12, 13) ; who was one of the assassins of Julius
Caesar ; and who, having afterwards joined Sextus Pompeius and
Antony, was executed by the order of Augustus after the battle of
Actium. A line or two of his works, which seem to have embraced
Tragedies, Elegies and Satires, have been preserved by Varro and
Quintilian ; and a short poem on Orpheus was long believed to be his,
but has been shown to have been composed in the sixteenth century A.D.
See also a part of a letter of his quoted by Sueton. Aug. 4.

opuscula, 'the minor works', i.e. elegies. Cp. 19, 35.

4. *reptare* ' saunter '.

6. *tu, emphatic.*

7. *divitias* 'real wealth', i.e. a sufficiency.

8. *quid voveat nutricula* ' what more could an old nurse pray '. The
diminutive is half playfully affectionate, half contemptuous. For such
a prayer of a nurse for her charge see Pers. 2, 31—40 *Nunc Licini in
campos, nunc Crassi mittit in aedes : Hunc optent generum rex et regina :
puellae Hunc rapiant ! quidquid calcaverit hic, rosa fiat !*

alumno [alere] ' foster-child '.

9. *sapere* 'to appreciate' sc. literature and art. So of a too
critical taste, Mart. 1, 4, 4 *Crede mihi nimium Martia turba sapit.
qui possit* ' if he is one who '; a restrictive subj., R. 1692.

10. *valetudo* 'good health'. *valetudo* is a neutral word, 'state of
health', and means bad or good according to the context.

11. *mundus* 'decent'. See 5, 6. Od. 3, 29, 14 *Mundaeque parvo
sub Lare pauperum Cenae.* Sat. 2, 2, 65 *Mundus erit qui non offendet
sordibus, atque In neutram partem cultus miser. crumena* 'money-bag';
cp. Juv. 11, 38 *Quis enim te deficiente crumena Et crescente gula manet
exitus ?*

12. *inter* repeated, cp. 2, 12.

14. *superveniet* 'will come as an unexpected addition'.

15. *bene curata cute*, see 2, 29. The point is ' in spite of my fine com-
mendations of simple pleasures you will find me an Epicurean after all '.

16. For Horace's lapses from the Stoic precepts see 1, 18. The
Edd. quote for *porcum*, Cicero in Pison. § 37 *Epicure noster, ex hara*
(' pigstye ') *non ex schola.*

EPISTLE V.

[An invitation to Torquatus to a modest banquet conceived in somewhat the same spirit as Odes 1, 20; 4, 11. It is to be on the eve of the birthday of Augustus, i.e. 22 Sept.]

1. *Archiacis lectis* 'couches made by Archias', some upholsterer at Rome who made plain but perhaps elegant furniture.

2. *cenare olus omne* 'to have a dinner entirely of vegetables'. The bare wants of men in the way of food according to Horace are *panis, olus, vinum*, Sat. 1, 1, 74. See also the preparations for the simple dinner of Scipio and Laelius, Sat. 2, 1, 75—6. Cp. Sat. 2, 2, 116—122; 2, 7, 30 *si nusquam es forte vocatus Ad cenam laudas securum olus.* Cp. Pers. 6, 19 *Solis natalibus est qui Tingat olus siccum muria.* Horace however can scarcely mean that the whole dinner is to be one plate of vegetables, which is his idea of the poorest fare, see 17, 13. He only wishes to warn his friend that he will have a simple dinner, what we call 'pot luck'. For *ceno* trans. cp. 15, 34.

3. *supremo sole* 'towards sunset'; whereas the usual time for the *cena* was the ninth hour, or about 3 P.M. On the 23rd September between one or two hours later than that would be verging towards sunset.

4. *iterum Tauro*, in the second consulship of Titus Statilius Taurus, B.C. 26.

diffusa 'draughted from the dolium into the amphora', equivalent to our 'bottled'. Cp. Juv. 5, 30 *Ipse capillato diffusum consule potat.* 11, 159 *Hic tibi vina dabit diffusa in montibus illis A quibus ipse venit.*

5. *Minturnas Sinuessanumque Petrinum.* Minturnae, on the Appian way about 3 miles from the sea on the rt. bank of the Liris. Sinuessa on the extreme South of Latium, also on the Appian way, close to the shore of the Sinus Caietanus. Near it were the celebrated Massic vineyards [*De Sinuessanis venerunt Massica prelis* Mart. 13, 111]. But the wine Horace alludes to was from an inferior vineyard on the *Rocca di Monte Ragone*, the Massic vines being to the South on the Campanian side.

6. *si melius quid habes* 'if you have any better wine to suggest, bring it, or submit to my orders' i.e. both as host and as master of the feast, cp. *regna vini*, Od. 1, 4, 18; *arbitrium bibendi*, Od. 2, 7, 25.

For the practice of guests contributing something to the banquet, see Od. 4, 12, 13—20.

7. *munda.* See on 4, 11. And cp. v. 21. Sat. 2, 4, 76—84 *Ten' lapides varios lutulenta radere palma Et Tyrias dare circum illota toralia vestes?*

8. *certamina divitiarum.* The same exhortation as in Od. 4, 12, 25 *Verum pone moras et studium lucri.*

9. *Moschi causam.* Porphyrion informs us that Moschus was a *rhetor* of Pergamum accused of poisoning, who was being defended by Torquatus and Asinius Pollio. The courts would not sit on this day, but still Torquatus might be busy with his case.

nato Caesare. Augustus was born on the 23rd of September, B.C. 63. Sueton. Aug. 4. Horace also celebrated Maecenas' birthday by a cena, see Od. 4. 11; and it was the custom at Rome to keep such days, whether the host's own or those of his friends or of public characters. Thus Antony is described as giving *natalicia* in honour of some one of his friends [Cic. Phil. 2, 6]. See also Juv. 12, 1. Pers. 1, 16. Mart. 7, 86.

11. *tendere noctem* etc. 'to lengthen out the summer night with kindly talk'. Cp. Od. 3, 21, 23 *Vivaeque producent lucernae Dum rediens fugat astra Phoebus.* Some difficulty has been felt in calling a night in late September a 'summer' night. But September is a hot and even dangerous season at Rome. Again it is suggested that Horace would not be in Rome in September; but he was kept there sometimes and perhaps on this occasion, see 14, 6.

12. *quo...uti* 'to what end give me good fortune if I may not use it?' Cp. Ov. Am. 2, 19, 7 *Quo mihi fortunam quae numquam fallere curet?* ib. 3, 4, 41 *Quo tibi formosam si non nisi casta placebat?* Heroid. 2, 53 *quo iam tot pignora nobis?*

13. *ob heredis curam* 'from regard to the interests of his heir'. *heredis* is an object genitive, cf. Od. 1, 12, 50 *tibi cura magni Caesaris data.* The saving only for an heir to inherit and use is a common thought, Od. 2, 3, 19 *extructis in altum Divitiis potietur heres.* 4, 7, 19 *Cuncta manus avidas fugient heredis, amico Quae dederis animo.* 3, 24, 61 *Indignoque pecuniam Heredi properet.* Cp. Persius 6, 33 sq.

14. *adsidet insano* 'is next to a madman'. Cp. the opposite *dissidens,* 'differing in judgment from', Od. 2, 2, 18. The metaphor may, as some say, be drawn from the theatre, but it is an obvious one, not requiring so definite an allusion.

spargere flores, cp. Od. 3, 19, 21 *Parcentes ego dexteras Odi:
sparge rosas.* 3, 29, 1 *Tyrrhena regum progenies, tibi Non ante verso
lene merum cado, Cum flore, Maecenas, rosarum et Pressa tuis balanus
capillis Iamdudum apud me est.*

16. *dissignat.* This form and not *des-* is best supported by the
MSS. here and in Ter. Ad. 87 *illa quae antehac facta sunt omitto;
modo quid dissignavit!* The meaning is said to be 'to do something
remarkable' good or bad. Here then 'what wonders does not wine
work!' The original sense is perhaps *aperit* (Porphyr.) but this
secondary sense comes from the notion of 'pointing out'. Thus the
dissignator in 7, 6 is the man who shows people to their places in a
funeral, as in Plaut. Poen. pr. 19 it is the man who does the like in a
theatre.

ebrietas, not 'drunkenness' but, 'warmth of wine'. So *ebrius* in
Sat. 1, 4, 51 does not mean 'drunk'. Cp. Od. 1, 18, 4 *neque Mordaces
aliter diffugiunt sollicitudines. Quis post vina gravem militiam aut
pauperiem crepat?*

operta recludit 'does away with reserve'. *In vino veritas.* Ovid [A.
A. 1, 237] expresses almost exactly the same ideas and illustrates the
meaning of *operta*.

> *Vina parant animos, faciuntque caloribus aptos,*
>   *Cura fugit multo diluiturque mero.*
> *Tunc veniunt risus, tum pauper cornua sumit,*
>   *Tum dolor et curae rugaque frontis abit.*
> *Tunc aperit mentes aevo rarissima nostro*
>   *Simplicitas, artes excutiente deo.*

21. *imperor* 'it is my task', 'I accept the command': for
imperatur mihi. Cp. *invideor*, A. P. 56 (Or.).

22. *toral.* The *toralia* were not the coverings of the couches
(*vestes stragulae*), but hangings from it to the ground. Cp. Sat. 2, 4, 84
Et Tyrias dare circum inluta toralia vestes. Becker's *Gallus* p. 290.
mappa: napkins, sometimes elaborately worked, were supplied to the
guests, as was inevitable where fingers were freely used; and sometimes
we hear of their being purloined. Mart. 12, 29 *Hermogenes tantus
mapparum, Pontice, fur est, Quantus nummorum vix puto Massa
fuit.*

24. *ostendat tibi*, i.e. by being polished like a mirror. Cp. Ter. Ad.
3, 3, 74 *postremo tanquam in speculum in patinas, Demea, inspicere iubeo.*

25. *eliminet* 'take beyond the threshold', 'blab' [properly, 'to turn out of doors']. Cp. Mart. 1, 27 *Hesterna tibi nocte dixeramus, quincunces puto post decem peractos, cenares hodie, Procille, mecum. Tu factam tibi rem statim putasti et non sobria verba subnotasti; exemplo nimium periculoso.* Μισῶ μνήμονα συμπόταν, *Procille.* 10, 48, 21 *Accedunt sine felle ioci, nec mane timenda Libertas.*

ut par...pari depend also upon *procurare*; 'I will take care that the company is congenial': according to the proverb *pares cum paribus facillime congregantur*, Cic. de Sen. § 7.   See also Hor. Od. 17, 218. Aristot. Eth. 9, 3 ὅμοιον τῷ ὁμοίῳ φίλον.

Butram Septiciumque, unknown friends.

26. *Sabinum.* This Sabinus has been identified with Ovid's Aulus Sabinus (Am. 2, 18, 27) and others, but we have no means of knowing the truth.

28. *umbris* 'uninvited guests', who came with some of the invited guests as their shadows.   It seems that their place at table was decided a good deal by the quality of the guest who brought them, as in Sat. 2, 8, 21—2 the *umbrae* brought by Maecenas occupy the *lectus medius*, while in Juvenal 5, 17 the *umbra* who is a *cliens* is on the *imus. est locus.*   Horace has named a party of five: if his table was like the sigma of Martial (10, 48, 5) there was room for seven, and to have more than three on each couch was vulgar; see Cic. in Pis. § 67.

30. *quotus esse velis* 'what fraction of the party you wish to be', i.e. of how many you wish the party to consist.   Or. quotes Mart. 14, 217 *Dic quotus et quanti cupias cenare.*

rebus omissis 'throwing all other business aside'.   So *relictis rebus* is used almost adverbially = 'exclusively'.   Cp. Ter. Haut. 840 *mihi nunc relictis rebus inveniundus est aliquis.*   Cic. Ep. Fam. 12, 14, 1.

31. *atria...postico.* The atrium was the first hall or saloon in a large Roman house after passing the vestibulum, with an opening in the roof.   It served as the place of waiting and reception for clients and others.   It would be entered through the front door or *ostium*: Horace therefore advises his friend to slip out by a back door opening into a side street.   Becker [*Gallus*, p. 242] quotes Plautus Stich. 3, 1, 40

est etiam hic ostium
aliud posticum nostrarum harunce aedium.

EPISTLE VI.

[Addressed to one Numicius; an essay on the philosophic temperament.]

1. *nil admirari* 'to lose self-possession at nothing'. Though these words have often been adopted as a motto for a cynical indifference to all the marvels of nature, Horace did not mean them in that sense. They seem to have been taken from some tradition of the words of Pythagoras, see Plutarch de Audiendo 13 Πυθαγόρας ἐκ φιλοσοφίας ἔφησεν αὐτῷ περιγεγονέναι τὸ μηδὲν θαυμάζειν. By which he seems to mean that philosophy had fortified him against all the unexpected turns of fortune, and against a foolish fear of natural phenomena, such as we often read of as being caused by eclipses and such things.

The better or reverential wonder and awe of what is above us is not attacked in these words. 'Wonder', says Plato, 'is the sole origin of philosophy, and above all feelings befits a philosopher'. [Plat. Theaet. 155 D.] 'The man', says Carlyle, 'who does not habitually wonder and worship, were he President of innumerable Royal societies, and carried the whole Mécanique Céleste and Hegel's philosophy in his single head,—is but a pair of spectacles behind which there is no eye'.

3. *hunc solem* 'the sun above us there', as though pointing. Cp. Terence Haut. 410 *luciscit hoc!* 'the day is breaking up there!'; and so often in Terence and Plautus. R. §§ 1423, 1431.

4—5. *sunt qui...spectent*, see on 1, 77. The argument is 'Some people are free from the foolish fear caused by natural phenomena: though you may be one of these, yet how about the value you attach to the wealth produced by the earth, and the other common objects of ambition?'

momentis, see 10, 16.

6. *maris...Indos*, the Arabian Gulf and Indian Ocean, from which came pearls, purple dye and other objects valued by the wealthy.

7. *ludicra* the games, gladiatorial exhibitions, races and such pleasures.

plausus et amici dona Quiritis 'applause in the theatre [see Od. 1, 20, 3 *datus in theatro cum tibi plausus*, cp. Od. 2, 17, 25] and office or other honours bestowed by the citizens'. [*Hunc si mobilium turba Quiritium Certat tergeminis tollere honoribus* Od. 1, 1, 7.] For

Quiritis the sing. for plur. see Od. 2, 7, 3, where the singular for 'a citizen' occurs. *amici* 'favouring you'.

8. *quo...ore* 'in what spirit, with what feelings, and with how (unmoved) a countenance do you think such things should be viewed?' i.e. Do you think these things ought to affect you?

9. *miratur*, this shows the sense in which Horace means to use the word to express a foolish and unreasonable desire and admiration for what ought to be indifferent to a wise man.

10. *pavor* 'in both cases terror (of losing the desired object) excites and unmans the person so feeling'. Cp. 10, 31.

13—14. *spe* 'expectation'. *defixis oculis* 'with eyes fixed in astonishment'.

15—16. A philosopher who (as the Stoics) pushes his pursuit even of virtue beyond reasonable limits may be called unsound : and so also he who pursues justice too strictly may be called unjust, because *summum ius summa iniuria*, Cic. de Off. 1, 10.

17. *i nunc* 'after that go and'. A formula of ironical or contemptuous exhortation constantly used after a string of warning examples or maxims. See Ovid, Ep. 3, 26; 4, 127; 12, 204. A. A. 2, 636. Juvenal 10, 310. Mart. 2, 6, 1. Sometimes the *nunc* is omitted as in Ovid, Am. 3, 3, 1 and in the famous address to Hannibal in Juv. 10, 166 *i demens et saevas curre per Alpes.*

argentum et marmor vetus 'antique silver plate and statues'. Juv. 1, 76 *argentum vetus et stantem extra pocula caprum. aeraque et artes* 'bronzes and other works of art'. Od. 4, 8, 1

> *Donarem pateras grataque commodus,*
> *Censorine, meis aera sodalibus,*
> *Donarem tripodas, praemia fortium*
> *Graiorum.*

The plunder of Sicily and Greece in the second century B.C. had introduced the taste for antiques into Rome, and the extravagance with which it was pursued is testified throughout Roman literature.

18. *Tyrios colores* 'purple dyes', so often referred to as being used in the *vestes stragulae* [Sat. 2, 4, 84] as well as in clothes, and which were manufactured from shells found in the seas off Tyre, as well as in other places. *cum gemmis* 'jewelled cups'. Or. quotes Verg. G. 2, 506 *Ut gemma bibat et Sarrano dormiat ostro.* Cp. Mart. 11, 11, 5 *Te potare decet gemma, Sardanapale.* id. 14, 109 *Gemmatum Scythicis ut luceat*

ignibus aurum Aspice? Cp. Juv. 5, 41 where the suspicious host set a
slave *Qui numeret gemmas, ungues observet acutos.*

21. *emetat agris = metat ex agris, emetat* not occurring elsewhere in
classical Latin (Or.).

22. *Mutus,* probably a real person who had obtained landed
property as his wife's dowry, but we don't know who he was.

indignum 'oh! shame!' *quod sit* ' seeing that he is'.

23. *mirabilis* ' an object of envious admiration'.

24. *quidquid sub terra* etc. 'time brings all things to light (*in
apricum,* 'into the sunlight'), and will return them in their glory to the
earth again'. Cp. Od. 1, 34 *valet ima summis Mutare, et insignem
attenuat Deus Obscura promens.* Horace is probably thinking of some
philosophical sentence such as that quoted by Or. from Xenophanes ἐκ
γῆς γὰρ τάδε πάντα καὶ ἐς γῆν πάντα τελευτᾶ. The sentiment is often
repeated in literature, see especially Soph. Aj. 646.

26. *porticus Agrippae,* the covered walk erected by M. Agrippa, the
great minister of Augustus, in B.C. 24, called the *porticus Neptuni,* and
decorated with pictures of the Argonauts. It was meant as a memorial
of the battle of Actium. See Mart. 3, 20, 11 *An spatia carpit Argonau-
tarum?*

via Appi, the road constructed in the Censorship of Appius Claudius
Caecus, B.C. 312—308, from Rome to Capua, and afterwards extended
to Brundusium. See 18, 20.

27. Cp. Od. 4, 7, 15 *Nos ubi decidimus, Quo pater Aeneas quo
Tullus dives et Ancus, Pulvis et umbra sumus. Numa* and *Ancus,* two
of the twelve kings.

28—66. If we are suffering physically we take measures to get
relief: if we want to secure mental happiness we should make up our
minds what will give it, and strain after that before everything.

30. *fortis* 'with resolute disregard of pleasure'. *si virtus,* the
Stoic doctrine. *omissis...deliciis,* cp. 5, 30 *rebus omissis.*

31. *verba putas* 'if on the other hand you think virtue mere words,
as a grove is a mere collection of timber'. This is a sufficient sense,
though some see a reference to sacred groves: 'If you think virtue
empty words, and groves mere timber without anything sacred in
them'. Brutus after Philippi exclaimed (Dio 57, 49) ὦ τλῆμον ἀρετή,
λόγος ἄρ' ἦσθα, ἐγὼ δέ σε ὡς ἔργον ἤσκουν.

32. *cave ne* 'see that you are the first in the market everywhere'.

33. *Cibyratica,* Cibyra a town in Phrygia, where there were great

iron works. *Bithyna* 'of Bithynia', a district in Asia on the South
Eastern coast of the Black Sea, in which much trade was done. Od.
3, 7, 3 *Thyna merce beatum.* Od. 1, 35, 7 *Quicumque Bithyna lacessit
Carpathium pelagus carina.*

35. *et quae pars quadret acervum* 'and another thousand to make up
the sum to four thousand'. Cp. Pers. 6, 77 *Rem duplica. Feci: iam tri-
plex, iam mihi quarto, Iam deciens redit in rugam: depinge, ubi sistam.*

36. *scilicet* 'for of course', ironical.

38. *bene nummatum* 'well supplied with money'. The word,
though in form a participle, must be regarded as an adjective. Cicero
(de leg. agr. 2, 22, 59) has also used the word, but apparently in jest,
and it is doubtful whether it is not as unauthorised as our 'monied'
'talented', and other such.

Suadela 'persuasiveness'. So Ennius, quoted by Cic. de Sen. 50
suadae medulla.

39—48. Contain practical suggestions (ironically made) on the
understanding that money is the secret of happiness.

39. *Cappadocum Rex*, Archelaus. Of his predecessor Cicero [Att.
6, 1, 4] said *nihil illo regno spoliatius, nihil rege egentius.*

40. *ne fueris hic tu* 'don't make the same mistake'. *hic*, see 15, 42.

chlamydes. The story is introduced ironically as an instance of how
much wealth can be accumulated by one man. 'Here's the sort of
thing', he would say, 'at which you should aim;—wealth beyond its
owner's calculation'. The *chlamys* was a Greek mantle consisting of
'an oblong piece of cloth to each side of which a gore (πτέρυξ) was
attached', and fastened on the shoulder or under the chin with a brooch.
It was regularly used at Athens as a riding cloak, but was sometimes
adopted also by Romans (Cic. Rabir. 10). Rich, s.v.

41. *praebere* 'supply' as a loan. They were probably wanted for
some procession.

42. *qui*, used (1) abl. with *cum, se quicum.* (2) as a subst. relat.
(3) as adverbial relative, as here, see 16, 63. R. 379.

44. *tolleret* 'let him (i.e. the praetor or whoever was giving the
games) take'. The imperf. subj. in oratio obliqua represents the present
imperative in oratio recta. The secondary tense is used because the
whole sentence is historical, depending upon *scribit* which is an historical
present. R. 1783, 1785.

47. Repeated from v. 2, to contrast the various ideas current on the
subject with his own definition.

S. H.   7

res 'wealth'. Cp. 1, 65.

49. *species et gratia* 'outward show (such as the emblems of office) and popularity'. The *gratia* will obtain the *species* by winning us office.

50. *servum*, a nomenclator to tell us the names of everyone, so that we may become popular by appearing to know everyone. Such an attendant was especially wanted by a candidate for office. Cicero employed one [Att. 4, 1, 5], and urges on his brother that to know the names of his supporters was the first and most necessary step in a canvass [de petit. § 25—32]. Plutarch tells us that one great cause of the popularity of Themistocles at Athens was that he was able to call all the citizens by their names [Plutarch. Them. 5]. For other uses of the *nomenclator*, see Juv. 1, 97—9, and Prof. Mayor's notes.

51. *qui fodicet* 'to nudge us'. For constr. see 4, 3. *trans pondera* 'across heavy goods', or loads in the street. Cp. Juv. 3, 240—256 for the obstacles in the Roman streets. The candidate reaches over intervening obstacles to shake hands with a powerful voter. Many other explanations have been given of the words *trans pondera.* (1) Orelli explains them to mean 'over the weights' on a shop counter, as though the candidate went into the various shops and shook hands over the counter with the shopmen. This seems too confined a meaning. (2) 'Over the stepping stones', which, as in the streets of Pompeii, took the place of our crossings. There is however no evidence of this meaning of *pondera.* (3) 'Leaning forward so as to overbalance himself'. This is the view of most recent authorities, including the late Dr Munro, in his note to Lucret. 6, 574. The objection to it is the peculiar use of *trans.*

52. *Fabia...Velina*, two of the 35 tribes of Rome. Though Horace uses the old republican illustration of a candidate trying to win over the electors, popular election had in his time become nearly formal, the chief officers being really nominated by Augustus, though he affected to preserve the rights of voters and 'recommend' candidates.

53, 54. *fasces...curule ebur* 'the bundles of rods and axes and the ivory chair', the symbols of the higher magistrates, Consul, Praetor and Aedile.

54. *frater, pater.* For the first as a complimentary title, see Juv. 5, 135 *vis, frater, ab ipsis Ilibus?* For the latter, see Verg. Aen. 5, 532 *sume, pater.* Hor. Sat. 2, 1, 12 *cupidum, pater optime, vires Deficiunt.* Cp. 7, 37.

55. *facetus* 'politely', opposed to *rusticus*; cp. *infaceto est infacetior rure* Catull. 22, 14. Horace uses it with the idea of satirical wit, the satirist Lucilius is *facetus Emunctae naris* (S. 1, 4, 7): with the notion of vulgar affectation S. 1, 2, 26: but, with a better sense of smiling grace, *molle atque facetum Vergilio annuerunt gaudentes rure Camenae* (S. 1, 10, 44).

56. *lucet* 'it is daylight', let us go at once for fish or game, even though we are reduced to the subterfuge of Gargilius, and purchase the boar which we pretend to have killed, thereby showing that we care not for the sport but for the luxury of the food.

61. *crudi tumidique lavemur.* The proper course was to go to the bath first and then to the cena. It seems however to have been the fashion among gourmands to go to the bath after the cena in search of a second appetite, a practice regarded as especially unhealthy. Cp. Pers. 3, 98 *Turgidus hic epulis atque albo ventre lavatur, Gutture sulfureas lente exhalante mefites: Sed tremor inter vina subit, calidumque trientem Excutit e manibus, dentes crepuere retecti, Uncta cadunt laxis tunc pulmentaria labris. Hinc tuba, candelae.* Cp. Juv. 1, 143.

62. *Caerite cera digni* 'deserving to be disfranchised'. The people of Caere in Etruria were one of the earliest states to be admitted to a curtailed Roman citizenship; hence *tabulae Caerites* came to be the name for the lists of disfranchised citizens.

63. *remigium Ulixi* 'the crew of Ulysses', turned into swine by Circe, see 2, 23.

64. *interdicta voluptas*, the slaughtering and eating the cattle of the Sun, Hom. Odyss. 12, 297—365, and the eating of the Lotus 9, 91—97.

65. *Mimnermus*, of Colophon or Smyrna, who flourished about B.C. 620—600, was an elegiac poet, whose works were chiefly amatory, their morality apparently of the complexion indicated by Horace. The first fragment as given by Bergk sufficiently explains Horace's words.

> Τίς δὲ βίος, τί δὲ τερπνὸν ἄτερ χρυσᾶς Ἀφροδίτης;
> τεθναίην, ὅτε μοι μηκέτι ταῦτα μέλοι,
> κρυπταδίη φιλότης καὶ μείλιχα δῶρα καὶ εὐνή.

67. *vive vale*, an amplification of the common *vale* at the end of letters. Cp. Sat. 2, 5, 110.

68. *candidus*, see on 4, 1. *si non his utere.* Or. quotes Plaut. Epid. 2, 2, 80 *immo si placebit utitor consilium si non placebit reperitote rectius.*

EPISTLE VII.

[A letter addressed to Maecenas, excusing the poet from attendance in Rome on the ground of health, and claiming a proper independence.]

1. *rure = ruri.* 'Rare except with adjective', R. 1170: cp. 14, 10.

2. *Sextilem.* This month was not called *August* until B.C. 8—7. Augustus succeeded Lepidus as Pontifex Maximus in B.C. 13, and in virtue of that office caused among other things a rectification of the Calendar; but the change of the name of *Sextilis* to *Augustus* seems not to have taken place until after his expedition in Gaul (B.C. 9) in which he received the submission of the Sicambri, on which occasion he honoured Tiberius with the imperial title and triumphal robes, and extended the boundaries of the Pomoerium. He chose the month of August rather than that of his birth (September) because in it he had first obtained the Consulship (B.C. 43) and won his greatest victories. Suet. Aug. 31.

mendax 'false to my promise'. *desideror* 'I am absent'.

5—6. *dum ficus—atris* 'while the season of the early fig and the heat surrounds the undertaker with his black-clothed mutes'. September was the unhealthy season in Rome, see 16, 16. Cp. Juv. 4, 56 *letifero autumno.* The South wind at that season was specially unhealthy, Hor. Sat. 2, 6, 18 *nec plumbeus Auster Autumnusve gravis Libitinae questus acerbae.* Cp. Juv. 6, 517. Suet. Ner. 39 *pestilentia unius autumni qua triginta funerum millia in rationem Libitinae venerunt.*

lictoribus, used for any 'attendants'. Or. quotes Cic. de Legg. 2 § 61 *dominus funeris citatus accenso et lictoribus.* For *dissignatorem,* see 5, 16.

7. *matercula* 'doting mother'. The diminutive is used to indicate a half contemptuous pity for the anxious or sorrowing mother.

8. *officiosa sedulitas,* constant performance of the duty of clients to their patrons in paying visits and conducting them to and from the forum. This was not only done by servile flatterers and legacy hunters (Sat. 2, 5, 47), but by all men under any tie of obligation either social or political. See Cicero's view of this practice, which he regards as the only return possible for men of humble means to their rich patrons, pro Mur. § 70.

opella forensis 'the various petty affairs of the forum': contemptuous diminutive.

9. *febres,* the agues which were prevalent at this season; cp. Juv.

4, 57 *iam quartanam sperantibus aegris. resignat* 'unseals', 'causes to be opened', i.e. on the death of the testators.

10. *quodsi* 'but whenever' or 'as soon as'. Cf. Sat. 2, 3, 10 *Voltus erat...praeclara minantis Si vacuum tepido cepisset villula tecto.*

inlinet 'sprinkles upon'. Horace is at his farm in the Sabine valley, at the first appearance of snow he means to go down to the sea coast. He did not like cold, see 20, 24.

12. *contractus*, various explanations have been given of the word. (1) 'huddled-up' to escape the cold [Or.], (2) 'rejoicing in retirement', (3) 'living frugally'. I think it means only 'shutting myself up', both on account of the season and the desire for study. Cp. Pers. 1, 13 *scribimus inclusi.*

15. *sodes*, see on 1, 62.

16. *benigne* 'no, thank you', a formula generally of polite refusal. The full phrase is *benigne dicis*. Plaut. Truc. 1, 2, 32. Ter. Phorm. 1051.

20. *prodigus et stultus* 'it is only the prodigal and fool that gives what he does not value', i.e. from the mere prodigal love of spending. Cp. Thackeray, *Vanity Fair*, 'Thriftless gives not from a beneficent pleasure in giving, but from a lazy delight in spending'.

21. *seges* 'sowing', elsewhere 'the crop', Od. 3, 23, 7; infr. 87. Or. quotes the proverbial sentence *ut sementem feceris ita metes*, 'as you have sown so shall you reap', Cic. de Or. 2 § 261.

22. *dignis* 'for those who are worthy of his favour'. *paratus*, this nom. case *where the subject of the infin. is the same as that of the main verb* was imitated by the poets from the usual Greek construction, cp. Od. 3, 27, 73 *uxor invicti Iovis esse nescis*. Catull. 4, 1 *Phaselus ille quem videtis, hospites, Ait fuisse navium celerrimus*. Verg. Aen. 2, 377 *sensit medios delapsus in hostes.*

23. *nec tamen*, yet is quite aware of the true value of things, and does not give from ignorance of it.

aera lupinis, a proverb from the beans used for money in the stage (*comicum aurum*), and as counters in games of chance.

24. *pro laude merentis* 'in proportion to (in a manner worthy of) the reputation of my benefactor' i.e. of you, Maecenas. *merentis = bene merentis.*

26. *forte latus* 'my strong frame'. For the use of *latus* cp. Od. 3, 10, 19 *Non hoc semper erit liminis aut aquae Caelestis patiens latus.* 3, 27, 26 *latus credidit tauro.*

angusta fronte 'on a forehead made narrow by clustering curls': something of the beauty on which Horace compliments Lycoris, Od. 1, 33, 5 *Insignem tenui fronte Lycorida.* Cp. Chaucer, *Miller's Tale,* ' Ful smal y-pulled weren hir browes two'.

27.   *dulce,* cp. *Dulce ridentem Lalagen amabo Dulce loquentem* Od. 1, 22, 23. These infinitives *loqui, ridere, maerere* are used properly as indeclinable verbal substantives. R. 1342. Cp. *hoc vivere triste* Pers. 1, 9. *ridere meum* id. 122. *meminisse iacet* Lucr. 4, 765.

28.   *fugam,* cp. Od. 1, 9, 21 *Nunc et latentis proditor intimo Gratus puellae risus ab angulo.* Verg. Ecl. 3, 64 *Malo me Galatea petit lasciva puella : Et fugit ad salices, et se cupit ante videri.*

Cinarae, cp. Od. 4, 1, 3 *Non sum qualis eram bonae sub regno Cinarae.* See on 14, 33.

protervae ' roguish', cp. Od. 1, 19, 7 *grata protervitas* (Or.).

29.   *volpecula.* This was altered to *nitedula* [= mouse] by Bentley, on the ground that foxes don't eat corn and could not get in through an *angusta rima.* But the fox as a personage in fables plays many unnatural parts, as for instance in the famous case of the sour grapes, and it is not safe to criticise a fable by the light of natural truth. The MSS. show no variation, and the fable is referred to by the Scholiast as *fabula vulpeculae.*

30.   *cumera,* a basket or tub with convex cover for keeping corn, used apparently only by those who kept corn in small quantities. Sat. 1, 1, 53 *cur tua plus laudes cumeris granaria nostris ?*

32.   *procul* 'hard-by', 'standing a little way off'. Cp. Verg. G. 4, 353; Aen. 2, 42.

34.   *si...imagine* ' If I am taunted by the application of this fable to myself '. *Compello* has a sense of rudeness, cp. Sat. 2, 3, 297. *resigno,* Od. 3, 29, 55 *si (fortuna) celeres quatit Pennas, resigno quae dedit.*

35.   *plebis somnum* ' the placid sleep which the common people obtain from simple fare', cp. Od. 3, 1, 21 *somnus agrestium Lenis virorum non humiles domus Fastidit. satur altilium* ' full-fed with fatted birds'. The *altilis* (alo) was a bird fatted in darkness and heat. See Mayor on Juv. 5, 115. *Satur* takes ablat. or gen., as *plenus.* R. 1336, 1339.

36.   *Arabum.* The supposed wealth of Arabia (felix) was pro-verbial, see Od. 1, 29, 1 ; 3, 24, 1 : by a common error which makes people think that the country from which articles of expensive luxury come must be necessarily rich.

muto takes the acc. or abl. of the thing given or taken in exchange; here the thing to be taken is in the abl. On the other hand the cases are reversed in Od. 1, 17, 1 *Velox amoenum saepe Lucretilem Mutat Lycaeo Faunus.*

37. *verecundum* 'modest' in making requests. Cp. 17, 43—45. *rexque paterque Audisti coram* 'you have been addressed to your face by me as 'father' and 'king'.' For *pater*, cp. 6, 54; for *rex*, cp. 17, 43. The latter was commonly applied to a patron, cp. Juv. 5, 14 *imputat hunc rex Et quamvis rarum tamen imputat.* Perhaps Horace may have used it also to Maecenas in reference to his supposed royal descent, Od. 1, 1, 1 *Maecenas atavis edite regibus.* For *audisti* see on 16, 17.

40—1. *Telemachus*, see Hom. Odyss. 4, 601, the speech of Telemachus is represented more faithfully than usual.

> ἵππους δ' εἰς Ἰθάκην οὐκ ἄξομαι, ἀλλὰ σοὶ αὐτῷ
> ἐνθάδε λείψω ἄγαλμα· σὺ γὰρ πεδίοιο ἀνάσσεις
> .   .   .   .
> ἐν δ' Ἰθάκῃ οὔτ ἄρ δρόμοι εὐρέες οὔτε τι λειμών·
> .   .   .   .
> οὐ γὰρ τις νήσων ἱππήλατος οὐδ' εὐλείμων.

42. *spatiis*, see 14, 9.

43. *Atride.* Telemachus is speaking to Menelaus, and begins (Odyss. 4, 594) with Ἀτρείδη (voc.).

45. *Tibur*, Tivoli, from which Horace's farm was not far distant. *vacuum* 'not crowded' as Rome is. *imbelle Tarentum*, cp. Sat. 2, 4, 34 *molle Tarentum*. It was one of the places Horace regarded as a possible retreat for his old age, Od. 2, 6, 11.

46—95. The folly of lifting a man by a sudden stroke of favour above his position into an employment unsuited to him illustrated by the tale of rich Philippus and the auctioneer. This episode has been closely imitated by Swift in his 'Address to the Earl of Oxford' 1713, beginning

> 'Harley, the nation's great support,
> Returning home one day from court,
> (His mind with public cares possest,
> All Europe's bus'ness in his breast.)
> Observed a Parson near Whitehall
> Cheap'ning old Authors at a stall.'

46. *Philippus*, L. Marcius Philippus, Cons. B.C. 91, was a great orator, next in reputation to Crassus and Antonius [Cic. Brut. 47]. He died about B.C. 76.

47. *octavam* 'about two o'clock', which was late for leaving off business: the law courts began about 9 and business generally seems to have ended at 1 P.M. *Septima finis erit*, Mart. 4, 8, 4, from 1 to 3 being devoted to exercise and the bath, followed by the *cena* at 3.

48. *Carinas.* A street from the S. E. end of the Forum led to the district on the Mons Oppius called *Carinae* where the church of S. Pietro in Vincoli now stands and the ruins of the baths of Titus. It was at this time a fashionable quarter.

50. *adrasum*, see on 15, 25. *vacua in umbra* 'in the booth of a barber now empty', because it was so late in the day that the customers and loungers were dispersed to dinner. The barber's shop has always been the resort of loungers, see Aristoph. Av. 1441, Plutus 338.

51. *proprios* 'his own nails', instead of being operated upon by the barber. Or. quotes Plautus Aul. 2, 4, 33 *quin ipsi pridem tonsor ungues dempserat. leniter* 'leisurely'.

52. *Demetri*, a Greek slave name.

53. *accipiebat* 'used to receive and carry out'.

unde domo 'where he lives' = *ex qua domo* : in this phrase *domo* seems to define and limit the more general *unde*. Cp. Verg. Aen. 8, 114 *Qui genus? unde domo?* quoted by Or.

55. *Volteium Menam.* The latter is a common slave name. The man was therefore probably a freedman who had taken as usual the praenomen of his patronus.

57. *loco* 'at the proper time'. Cp. Od. 4, 12, 28 *Dulce est desipere in loco.* It seems better to make the infinitives *properare, cessare* ('to take his ease'), *quaerere, uti* depend upon *narrat* rather than on *notum* (cp. 6, 25).

quaerere et uti = *quaerere et quaesitis uti*, 'both to seek gain and enjoy it when obtained'. Cp. 15, 32.

58. *lare certo* 'a settled home'. Cp. 15, 28.

59. *Campo* 'in the Campus Martius' as a place of exercise. Od. 1, 8, 3 *cur apricum Oderit Campum.* Infr. 11, 4. The sports of the Campus are mentioned in the A. P. 379, *Ludere qui nescit campestribus abstinet armis, Indoctusque pilae discive trochive quiescit.* Cp. Sat. 1, 6, 126.

61. *credere, mirari*, for this use of the infinitive (only the present

tense) to *express action without marking definite time*, sometimes called the historic infinitive, see R. 1359.

62. *benigne*, supr. l. 16. Mena thinks that he is being hoaxed, and cannot believe that he is really invited; he gets out of it therefore by refusing: cp.

> 'Swift seem'd to wonder what he meant
> Nor would believe my Lord had sent;
> So never offered once to stir,
> But coldly said, *Your Servant, Sir.*'

63. *neget*, dubitative subj. 'Can it be that he refuses?'
inprobus 'persistently', cp. *labor improbus* Verg. Georg. 1, 146.

65. *vendentem*, at an auction. *tunicato*, wearing the short close-fitting tunic, i.e. not the *toga*, as the better class of Romans would do in the city: though at this time the upper classes were beginning to drop the use of the heavy *toga*; a custom which Augustus in vain tried to withstand. Suet. Aug. 40.
popello 'humble folk', cp. *plebecula* Ep. 2, 1, 186.

66. *occupat* 'surprises him', φθάνει. Cp. 6, 32.
salvere iubet 'says salve! to him', the ordinary greeting on a first meeting.

67. *excusare* 'to allege as an excuse'. Cp. the construction of *defendere*. Orelli quotes Cic. Phil. 9, 38 *excusare morbum.*

68—9. *venisset...providisset*, subj. in oratio obliqua. *mane*, as a salutator, or morning caller, the time for whom was from the first to the third hour. Cp. Mart. 4, 8 *Prima salutantes atque altera conterit hora.* id. 1, 55, 6 *Et matutinum portat ineptus Ave.*

69. *providisset* 'seen him first'. Orell. quotes Plaut. Asin. 2, 4, 44 *non hercle te provideram, quaeso ne vitio vertas*, 'don't put a bad interpretation on it'.
sic...si 'on this condition, that'. *si cenas*, the protasis has an indicative verb where the apodosis is imperative. R. 1571.

71. *post nonam*, cp. Mart. 4, 8, 6 *Imperat extructos frangere nona toros.* As the cena divided the day the *nona* gave rise to our word 'noon'.
rem auge, cp. 6, 47; 16, 68. *strenuus*, 2, 70.

72. *dicenda tacenda* 'things of all sorts, indifferent or confidential', such as won't bear to be repeated in the morning, see 5, 25.

73—75. Cp. Swift's paraphrase:

> 'The Doctor now obeys the summons,
> Likes both his company and commons;
> Displays his talent, sits till ten;
> Next day invited comes again:
> Soon grows domestick, seldom fails
> Either at morning, or at meals;
> Came early, and departed late:
> In short, the Gudgeon took the bait.'

75. *mane.* See on l. 68.

76. *rura suburbana* 'to his patron's country seat in the neighbourhood of Rome', in the Sabine territory, as is shown in v. 77. It is without *ad* following the construction of *rus.*

indictis Latinis, on the day of the *feriae Latinae*, which were not on a fixed day (*statae*), but on a day appointed (*indictus*) each year by the Consul (*conceptivae*). The busy Roman of the upper class often took the opportunity of going during the holiday to his country house, either to keep aloof from the festival or to attend it more conveniently, as it was on the Alban Mount in commemoration of the confederacy of the Latin States.

77. *impositus mannis* 'riding in the carriage drawn by Gallic horses'. Cp. the use of *equi* for 'chariot' in Od. 3, 3, 15 *hac Quirinus Martis equis Acheronta fugit.* Verg. G. 2, 358 *invectus equis.* Others explain it as 'riding on Gallic horses'. The point however seems to be that Philippus takes Mena with him in his chariot to amuse himself with his novel expressions of admiration of the country, which the town-bred auctioneer had not seen before.

80. *septem sestertia* 'seven thousand sestertii', about £56.

81. *agellum* 'a small farm', cp. 14, 1.

83. *ex nitido* 'from a dapper townsman'. The epithet given by Juvenal (3, 157) to a *praeco*: opposed to *sordidus* 'ill-clad', like a rustic.

84. *vineta crepat mera* 'his talk is all of vineyards': cp. for *crepat* Od. 1, 18, 5 *Quis post vina gravem militiam aut pauperiem crepat?* *sulcos* in which the vines were planted, see Od. 3, 1, 10.

ulmos 'elms for training vines upon'. See 16, 3 and cp. Od. 2, 15, 5. Poplars were also used for the same purpose, Epode, 2, 10.

85. *inmoritur studiis* 'almost kills himself in the ardour of his pursuit', 'works himself to death over'. The word seems not used elsewhere except in a literal sense of dying or wasting away.

senescit 'exhausts himself'.

87. *mentita.* Cp. Od. 3, 1, 30 *fundus mendax.*
enectus (enĕco) 'worn out'.

88. *media de nocte.* Cp. 2, 32.

90. *scabrum intonsumque*, contrasted with the man as he had first seen him *adrasum*, l. 50.

91. *durus attentusque* 'hardworking and unremitting in labour': cp. *tute attente illorum officia fungere* Ter. Haut. 66. For *durus* cp. 16, 70 and Sat. 1, 7, 6, where it = 'obstinate' 'persistent'.

92. *Pol* or *Edepol* 'by Pollux', an oath common to men and women, while *Hercle* was proper to men, and *Ecastor* to women.

miserum: worse than *durus* or *intentus.*

94. *quod te per Genium* 'Nay but I beg you in the name of your guardian God'. The ordinary form of a solemn adjuration: cp. Verg. Aen. 2, 141 *Quod te per superos et conscia numina veri...oro miserere laborum.*

quod = 'as to which'.

Genium. The Genius was the god especially connected with each individual from his birth (*gigno, genus*). He accordingly was especially worshipped on the birthday, Od. 3, 17, 14; Persius 2, 3 *Funde merum Genio*: and this worship was particularly common among country-folk, see Hor. Epist. 2, 1, 144.

96—99. The moral: A mistake of this sort should be retrieved as soon as possible.

99. *modulo ac pede* 'measure and foot rule'. *verum* 'right': cp. 12, 23.

EPISTLE VIII.

[Another letter to one of the staff of Tiberius mentioned in 3, 15, mostly on the poet's own state of mind.]

1. *Celso Albinovano.* See Introduction, § 3. *gaudere...refer* 'wish him joy and prosperity'.

2. *Neronis*, sc. of Tiberius, see on 3, 2.

3. *quid agam* 'how I am': cp. 3, 15. *minantem* 'promising myself that I will do': cp. Sat. 2, 3, 9 *Atqui vultus erat multa et praeclara minantis.*

4. *suaviter* 'to my own content'. *haud quia* 'not at all because'. *grando*, cp. Od. 3, 1, 29 *Non verberatae grandine vineae.*

5—8. The subjunctives *contuderit, aegrotet, velim, offendar, irascar* are accounted for by the sentences being oblique depending upon *refer* in v. 2. *momorderit* 'parch', used also of the effect of cold, Sat. 2, 6, 45.

6. *longinquis* 'at a great distance from town', as in the case of rich men with *latifundia* in different parts of Italy. Cp. Mart. 3, 58, 51 *Rus hoc vocari debet an domus longe?* 'a town house out of town'.

8. *quod levet* 'such as might relieve'. *aegrum* 'sick in mind', that is, in a bad state from evil passions. Cp. Sat. 2, 3, 162.

10. *cur*, sc. *irascar cur*, 'I ask them angrily why'. 'I am angry because'. Orelli compares Cic. Att. 3, 13, 2 *quod me saepe accusas, cur hunc meum casum tam graviter feram, debes ignoscere.*

11. Cf. Ovid Met. 7, 21 *video meliora proboque Deteriora sequor.*

12. *ventosus* 'changeable as the wind'. Cp. 19, 37.

13. *ut valeat* 'how he is'. *ut vales?* is the common form of greeting. See Terence Haut. 406.

rem gerat 'he is getting on with his official duties' as *scriba* to Tiberius.

14. *iuveni* 'the young prince'. *cohorti*, see on 3, 6.

15. *recte*, an ordinary and somewhat evasive answer. See Terence Haut. 228. Hecyr. 355. *gaudere* sc. *iubeas* 'wish him joy'.

16. *auriculis*, playful diminutive. Pers. 1, 107 *quid opus teneras mordaci radere vero Auriculas?* cp. Hor. Sat. 1, 9, 20.

17. We shall like you if your position does not induce you to give yourself airs. Cp. Od. 3, 27, 75 *ferre magnam fortunam* 'to rise to the height of your good fortune'.

EPISTLE IX.

[A letter of introduction addressed to Tiberius [see Ep. 3] in favour of the poet's friend Septimius, to whom Ode 2, 6 is addressed, and who appears to have been also intimate with Augustus [Sueton. Hor.]. The readers of the Cicero correspondence will know how frequently such introductions were asked for and given from men at Rome to officials in the provinces. So much a matter of course was it to give them that Cicero warns his friends not to take much notice of them unless he adds something out of the common way. It would be written in A.D. 20 about the same time as Epp. 3 and 1.]

1. *nimirum,* somewhat ironical, 'doubtless', as though Horace would suggest that Septimius made too much of this power with Tiberius. *unus* 'better than anyone else'.

3. *scilicet* [*sci* or *scire, licet*] 'as you may see', with a slight deprecatory or apologetic sense.

laudare 'recommend'. *tradere* 'introduce': cp. Sat. 1, 9, 45 *haberes Magnum adiutorem posset qui ferre secundas Hunc hominem velles si tradere.* Cp. infr. 18, 78.

4. *legentis* 'selecting'. *honesta = honestos homines,* but the poet wishes to put it in as general terms as possible.

5. *cum fungi censet,* in apposition to *cum rogat* etc., 'when he thinks that I am an intimate friend', lit. 'that I perform the function of a somewhat intimate friend'.

6. *valdius (validius,* cp. *caldior, soldum,* Sat. 1, 3, 52 ; 2, 5, 65), 'better', 'more clearly' than I myself.

8. *mea...putarer* 'lest I should be thought to have represented my influence as less than it was'.

11. *frontis...urbanae* 'assurance'. Orelli compares Cic. Fam. 5, 12, 1 *pudor quidam paene subrusticus.* Cp. also Cic. in Pis. 1, 1 *iamne sentis quae sit querella hominum frontis tuae?*

descendi ad praemia 'I have fallen back upon what is to be gained by assurance'. *descendere* in this sense means to 'adopt an alternative' which though not the best is the better of two. Many have taken the language as drawn from the arena: but this is I think rightly rejected by Orelli and Prof. Wilkins.

13. *scribe tui gregis* 'enroll in the list of your set', 'among the number of your intimates'. Cp. Cic. Fin. 1, § 65 *greges amicorum :* supra 4, 16: Ov. Tr. 4, 10, 48 *Dulcia convictus membra fuere mei.*

gregis, a partitive genitive.

EPISTLE X.

[Addressed to Aristius Fuscus (for whom see Introduction, § 3), from the country. Verses 1—21 contain a plea for the pleasures of the country as against those of the town. Verses 22—43, a number of maxims as to the true way of happiness, mostly warnings against an over anxious search for riches. 44—50 He concludes with asking for similar advice from Fuscus in case he acts inconsistently with his preaching.]

1. *salvere iubemus,* cp. 7, 66.

3. *gemelli,* affectionate or playful diminutive of *gemini.*

4—5. *fraternis,* cp. 3, 35. *quidquid negat* 'whatever the one denies the other denies also, and we agree thoroughly'. Cicero (de Am. § 15) says that the essence of friendship is *voluntatum, studiorum, sententiarum summa consensio.*

5. *vetuli notique columbi* 'like old and intimate stock-doves'. Horace often introduces a comparison in apposition, i.e. without any adverb or conjunction to mark it. Cp. 2, 42; 3, 34. The diminutive *vetuli* is again used playfully. For *noti* 'well known to each other', cp. Sat. 1, 1, 85 *Vicini oderunt, noti, pueri atque puellae.*

6. *nidum servas,* i.e. you cling to your home in town. Cp. 20, 21.

8. *quid quaeris?* An ordinary phrase dismissing further details and summing up.

vivo 'I really live', 'I enjoy life', cp. Mart. 2, 90 *Vivere quod propero pauper nec inutilis annis Da veniam; properat vivere nemo satis.* Cp. 1, 41. *regno* 'am as happy as a king', with a reference to the Stoic doctrine, see 1, 107; 18, 107.

9. *ad caelum fertis* 'you praise to the skies'. Some MSS. read *effertis,* which is the more common word in this connection. Cp. Cic. de Am. 24 *efferat laudibus:* ad Fam. 9, 14 *te summis laudibus ad caelum extulerunt.*

rumore secundo 'with everyone's consent to your praise', 'the popular talk being on your side'. *secundus* (sequor) = favourable, cp. Od. 1, 10, 23; 3, 11, 50.

10—11. 'Like a priest's runaway slave I refuse the rich sacrificial cakes which I might get in his service and prefer plain bread and liberty'. The priest represents the town life, the fugitive slave the poet, who hastens to the simpler life of the country. *mellitis placentis* 'honey cakes', cp. Mart. 5, 40, 3 *Hyblaeis madidus thymis placentas.* They could not have been large, for Porcius made himself ridiculous by swallowing them whole (Sat. 2, 8, 24).

12. *vivere naturae convenienter* 'to live in a manner agreeable to nature', referring to the Stoic definition of the *summum bonum,* i.e. *secundum naturam vivere:* cp. Cic. de Am. § 19 *naturam optimam bene vivendi ducem.* So also de Sen. § 24.

13. *ponendae domo* 'for placing your house'. Observe *domo = domui,* dat.

15—16. *est ubi.* Horace seems to have in his mind the words put in the mouth of Socrates in Xenophon Oecon. 5, 9, χειμάσαι δὲ πυρὶ ἀφθόνῳ καὶ θερμοῖς λουτροῖς ποῦ πλείων εὐμάρεια ἢ ἐν χώρῳ; ποῦ δὲ ἥδιον θερίσαι ὕδασί τε καὶ πνεύμασι καὶ σκιαῖς ἢ κατ᾽ ἀγρόν; *plus=magis*, cp. Cic. de Sen. § 27 *vires adulescentis...non plus quam tauri desiderabam*.

tepeant 'are mild and warm'. Cp. Sat. 1, 4, 30 *sol quo Vespertina tepet regio.* Od. 2, 6, 17 *Ver ubi longum tepidasque brumas Iupiter praebet.*

16. *Canis...Leonis.* The sun enters Leo on the 20th July and the dog-star (*canicula*) rises on the same day but is not apparent until July 26.

momenta 'the swift movement', cp. 6, 4, as though the Lion were enraged by the heat. Cp. Od. 3, 29, 19 *furit...stella vesani Leonis.*

18. *somnos*, see on 7, 35.

19. *Libycis...lapillis* 'the tessellated floors of Libyan marble'. For African marble brought from the Numidian quarries, see Od. 2, 18, 4 *columnas ultima recisas Africa.* And for the marble tessellated floors, Od. 2, 14, 27 *mero Tinget pavimentum superbum.*

21. *trepidat* 'ever hastens'. Cp. Od. 2, 3, 11 *quid obliquo laborat Lympha fugax trepidare rivo?*

22. *nempe* 'why! even in' etc. *silva*, the shrubs were planted in the centre of the peristylium, with flowers, and fountains. Cp. Tibullus 3, 3, 15 *Et nemora in domibus sacros imitantia lucos.*

23. *domus...agros* 'a town house which commands a wide view of the country'.

25. *mala perrumpit furtim fastidia* 'will force its way insensibly through vicious pride', i.e. recur inevitably to a simpler life. *furtim*, the metaphor seems taken from the unperceived growth of a tree which gradually forces itself through the strongest obstacles, walls, masonry or the like. Cp. Juv. 10, 145 *saxis...ad quae Discutienda valent sterilis mala robora fici.* Cp. Pers. 1, 25; Mart. 10, 2, 9.

26—29. A merchant who could not distinguish Tyrian from Italian purple would lose: so will a man who does not know true from false.

26. *contendere ostro* 'to compare it with'. *ostro* is dat. For the active sense of *contendere* cp. Cic. de N. D. 33 § 10 *patere igitur rationem meam cum tua contendere*, 'allow me to compare my method with yours'.

Sidonio='Tyrian', see 6, 18.

88 *EPISTLES OF HORACE.* I.

27. *Aquinatem fucum* 'dye from Aquinum', an inferior dye. *potantia,* cp. Mart. 2, 29, 3 *Quaeque Tyron totiens epotavere lacernae.*

28. *propriusve medullis* 'or more vital', 'nearer to a vital part'. Cp. Juv. 14, 215 *nondum implevere medullas Maturae mala nequitiae.*

30—32. Cp. 6, 8—9. *plus nimio* 'more than too much', 'extravagantly'. Horace uses the same expression in Od. 1, 18, 15; 1, 33, 1.

31. *mirabere,* see on 6, 1. *pones* 'you will give them up', = *depones;* opposed to *colligere* in A. P. 160.

33. *reges* 'to outstrip in the true enjoyment of life kings and kings' friends'. Cp. Verg. G. 4, 132 *Regum aequabat opes animis.* In both cases *reges* = 'the great'.

34. *cervus equum.* This fable is attributed to Stesichorus by Aristotle, Rhet. 2, 20. In Phaedrus (4, 3) the same fable occurs, but a wild-boar muddying the stream at which a horse drinks takes the place of the stag.

36. *opes* 'help', cp. 2, 136.

37. *victor violens* 'but when as conqueror he left his foe with wild plunges', βιαζόμενος. Taken in this way it adds point to the next line, for with all his plunging he could not shake his rider off. Several recent editors however have adopted a conjecture *victo ridens,* which I cannot like in spite of its ingenuity.

40. *caret* 'loses'. *inprobus* 'because morally unsound', as being without the temperance and self-control necessary for the support of every fortune in life.

42. *olim* 'at times', 'usually', cp. Sat. 1, 1, 25.

43. *uret* 'will gall'. Cp. 13, 6; 16, 47.

44. *vives,* the future is a polite imperative, cp. 13, 2 and index. *sapienter* 'as a wise man should'. *Aristi,* see Introduction, § 3.

45. *incastigatum* 'uncorrected'. The word is not used elsewhere. For *castigare* = 'to correct', see Pers. 1, 7.

46. *cogere* 'to collect'. So perhaps Od. 3, 3, 51 *aurum cogere humanos in usus.*

48. *digna sequi,* see on 3, 35. Money should be the slave, not the captor.

49. *dictabam* 'I am dictating' to my amanuensis. In letters the imperfect is usually employed to describe what the writer is doing; as he puts himself in the place of the recipient of the letter. The rule

of the 'epistolary imperfect' however is by no means uniformly observed in Cicero's letters. R. 1468.

post fanum putre Vacunae 'in the rear of the decaying temple of Vacuna'. A Sabine goddess of victory or war, who had had a temple near Horace's Sabine farm.

EPISTLE XI.

[Addressed to a friend unknown to us named Bullatius, who is travelling in Asia Minor and the adjacent Islands, warning him not to be so captivated by the pleasures of any of the towns there as to believe that they would be a happier place for permanent residence than Rome.]

1. *Chios, notaque Lesbos.* These islands were noted for their wine— see Epode 9, 34 *Et Chia vina aut Lesbia.* Cp. Od. 1, 17, 20; Sat. 2, 3, 115. And Lesbos was *nota* also as the home of Alcaeus, cp. Od. 1, 1, 34 *Lesboum barbiton*; 1, 26, 11 *Lesbio plectro*; 1, 32, 4 *Barbite... Lesbio primum modulate civi.*

2. *concinna Samos* 'pretty Samos'. Horace uses the word elsewhere always of speech or style, Sat. 1, 3, 50; 1, 10, 23; Epist. 2, 1, 74, = 'neat', 'elegant'. Cicero ad Q. F. 3, 1, 1 applies the epithet to the plaster (*tectorium*) on the walls of a villa. On the whole the epithet is not wholly complimentary to Samos, rather in a vein of patronage from a citizen of Rome to so insignificant a place. It alludes to its temples—especially that of Juno—and its scenery.

Croesi.—Croesus king of Lydia, of which the capital was Sardis, from B.C. 560 to 546, when he was captured and dethroned by Cyrus.

3. *Smyrna, Colophon,* two of the cities of Asia which claimed to be the birthplace of Homer.

4. *prae* 'in comparison with'. Cp. *veros illos Atticos prae se paene agrestes putat* Cic. Brut. § 286.

sordent 'seem poor', cp. 18, 18.

5. *venit in votum* 'attracts your desires', 'becomes an object of desire': cp. Sat. 2, 6, 1 *Hoc erat in votis.*

Attalicis ex urbibus 'one of the cities which once belonged to Attalus', king of Pergamum, who left his dominions to Rome B.C. 133.

7. *Scis, Lebedus quid sit.* Horace supposes Bullatius to answer. The town of Lebedus, once one of the 12 Ionian cities, was ten miles from the promontory of Mycolessus. It became deserted by the removal of its inhabitants to Ephesus by Lysimachus [about B.C. 300].

7. *Gabiis.* The ancient Latin town of Gabii was on the Via Praenestina about half way between Rome and Praeneste. It had long lost all its importance and was nearly deserted, except for a few visitors on account of its waters. Cp. 15, 9; Juv. 7, 3.

8. *Fidenis* (Castel Giubileo), in Latium five miles from Rome, on a hill overlooking the Tiber, was destroyed in B.C. 438, and remained in a semi-deserted state ever after.

9. *obliviscendus et illis* 'to be forgotten by them too'. The passive use of the gerundive of deponent verbs is common, and that *obliviscor* should have this usage is accounted for by its originally governing the accusative of the object, cp. *carendus, fruendus, utendus, fungendus.* See Roby vol. 2 p. lxxvii. *illis* dat. of the agent, regularly employed with gerundive. R. 1146. Cp. 19, 3.

10. *e terra* 'from the safe shore'. Cp. Lucr. 2, 1 *Suave mari magno motantibus aequora ventis E terra magnum alterius spectare laborem.*

11. *Capua.* Pr. § 121 C. From Capua to Rome a traveller followed the Via Appia.

12. *caupona* 'in a wayside inn'. Horace seems not to have found the inn-keepers to his taste along this road. See Sat. 1, 5, 4. And for the general inconveniences of the Italian inns, see 17, 8 and Mayor on Juv. 8, 161.

13. *frigus collegit* 'has contracted a chill'. So *colligere iram* 'to grow angry', A. P. 160. Orelli also quotes Ovid Met. 5, 446 *sitim colligere.*

16. *trans Aegaeum* 'on the other side of the Aegean', and so refuse to come home because you have been tossed on the sea once.

17. *incolumi* 'to a man of sound mind', i.e. one who is not led away by groundless fancies at the charms of these beautiful places.

Rhodos et Mytilene, cp. Od. 1, 7, 1 *Laudabunt alii claram Rhodon aut Mytilenen.* The Island of Lesbos is called Mitylene from its chief town.

facit 'does for one', i.e. they serve as temporary reliefs: cp. Ovid Her. 2, 39 *Per Venerem nimiumque mihi facientia tela*; 6, 128 *Medeae faciunt ad scelus omne manus*; 14, 56 *Non faciunt molles ad fera tela manus.*

16—19. *quod...Tiberis,* i.e. they are good for a special purpose, not for continuance. *paenula,* a loose overcoat without sleeves. *campestre* a kilt or running-drawers worn by gladiators and athletes; the name is derived from the Campus Martius being the most common place for athletic games, see 7, 59.

19.   *Tiberis,* i.e. for bathing, see Od. 1, 8, 8 *Cur timet flavum Tiberim tangere.*

20.   *dum licet* 'while we may', almost a mere commonplace to avoid too positive a statement, cp. Od. 2, 11, 16.

22.   *fortunaverit,* a word used especially in a religious sense, see the prayer in Pers. 2, 45 *da fortunare Penates !*

23.   *grata,* cp. Od. 1, 9, 14 *Quem sors dierum cunque dabit lucro Appone.*

in annum 'from year to year', see 2, 38.

25.   *si* 'if as is the case', 'seeing that'.   *aufert...currunt,* the rule is that if *si* has indic. in *apodosis* it has it also in *protasis.*

26.   *maris effusi arbiter* 'commanding a view of a wide sea'.

27.   *currunt,* cp. Sat. 1, 1, 29 *per omne audaces mare qui currunt.*

28.   *strenua inertia,* 'a busy idleness', which keeps us at work doing nothing or what is worth nothing.   Cp. Pliny Ep. 9, 6 *otiosissimae occupationes.*

navibus atque quadrigis, i.e. 'by travelling by sea and land'.

30.   *Ulubris* a deserted township of Latium near the Pomptine marshes.   Juv. 10, 102 *vacuis Ulubris.*

aequus 'unmoved by the chances of life'.   Cp. Od. 2, 3, 1

> *Aequam memento rebus in arduis*
> *Servare mentem, non secus in bonis*
> *Ab insolenti temperatam*
> *Laetitia.*

EPISTLE XII.

[Iccius is M. Vipsanius Agrippa's steward or agent (*procurator*) in Sicily.   This letter is written partly to recommend the poet's friend Grosphus, partly to advise his correspondent to be contented and not to neglect philosophy entirely for the sake of business.   That Iccius had been a student of philosophy we learn from Od. 1, 29, 10—16. The letter appears to have been written late in B.C. 19.   See v. 26—7.]

1.   *fructibus* 'the income arising from the property', either by way of rent or share of the produce: cp. Cic. ad Att. 11, 2 *in quos sumptus*

abeunt fructus praediorum. The farms were probably chiefly pastoral: see Od. 2, 16, 33.

2. *si recte frueris* 'if you avail yourself of rightly', i. e. if you use wisely the percentage which comes to you as procurator. *non est ut,* 'there can be no'. Cp. Od. 3, 1, 9 *Est ut viro vir latius ordinet Arbusta sulcis* (Or.).

4. *pauper* 'destitute', πτωχὸς as opposed to πένης (Arist. Plut. 552). *usus rerum = res*: cp. Od. 3, 1, 43 *usus purpurarum*; Verg. G. 2, 466 *usus olivi = olivum* nearly. Here there is special reference to the legal meaning of *usus* as opposed to ownership: see Ep. 2, 2, 138.

5. *lateri,* i.e. *si bene est* 'if your body is well', cf. 7, 26. *pedibus,* i.e. *si bene est* 'if your feet are sound', not touched by podagra. Some however explain these words as = 'if you have enough for clothes and shoes'; which Orelli seems to think absurd, but I think has something to be said for it.

7. *in medio positorum abstemius* 'abstaining from the luxuries within your reach': cp. Sat. 1, 2, 108 *transvolat in medio posita et fugientia captat.*

8. *urtica,* a kind of nettle used when young for flavouring salads, still used by the Italians. For Horace's vegetable diet see 5, 2.

9. *confestim* 'by a sudden shower of wealth'.

10. *nescit* 'is unable'. Od. 3, 13, 9 *Te flagrantis atrox hora caniculae Nescit tangere.*

12. *Democriti.* The Eleatic philosopher Democritus was born at Abdera about B.C. 460 and died about B.C. 357. Or. quotes Cic. de Fin. 5 § 87 *Democritus...qui certe ut quam minime a cogitationibus abduceretur patrimonium neglexit agros deseruit incultos.* He is sometimes called the laughing philosopher (γελασῖνος), as opposed to Heraclitus, who wept at the follies of mankind.

13. *peregrest* 'is abroad', i.e. in philosophical contemplation. Cp. Cic. pro Mil. § 33 *vestrae peregrinantur aures* (Or.). For the word see Sat. 1, 6, 102. Cp. Arist. Nub. 229 κρεμάσας τὸ νόημα καὶ τὴν φροντίδα λεπτὴν καταμίξας εἰς τὸν ὅμοιον ἀέρα. Cp. the phrases *penes te* Sat. 2, 3, 273; *apud me* Ter. Haut. 921.

14. *scabiem et contagia,* a metaphor taken from the pestilence in flocks, with which Iccius was now much concerned. Cp. Verg. Georg. 3, 298 *glacies ne frigida laedat Molle pecus, scabiemque ferat turpesque podagras.* Juv. 2, 78 *dedit hanc contagio labem Et dabit in plures; sicut grex totus in agris Unius scabie cadit et porrigine porci.*

15. *nil parvum sapias* 'indulge no petty thought'. For *sapere aliquid* representing a state of mind, cp. Pers. 1, 11 *cum sapimus patruos*.

adhuc 'still' in spite of your engrossing employments.

16—19. The subjects of speculation of the natural philosopher. Cp. Verg. G. 2, 475 *me...Musae...Accipiant, caelique vias et sidera monstrent, Defectus solis varios lunaeque labores: Unde tremor terris.*

18. *obscurum* proleptic 'so that it becomes dark'.

19. *rerum concordia discors* 'the harmony in apparent discord of the universe'. Or. quotes Seneca, Quaest. 7, 27, *tota haec mundi concordia ex discordibus constat.*

20. *Empedocles* of Agrigentum [fl. circ. B.C. 444], a Pythagorean philosopher. *Stertinius* was a Stoic, and is referred to in Sat. 2, 3, 33 in connection with the Stoic doctrine of the essential madness of all the non-wise, *insanis et tu, stultique prope omnes, Siquid Stertinius veri crepat:* hence *deliret.* ib. 296 he calls him the 'eighth wise man'. *Stertinium acumen = Stertinius acutus.* Names in *-ius* are used as adjectives.

21—22. But, whether Pythagorean or Stoic, be friendly with Pompeius Grosphus.

seu pisces...trucidas 'whether you murder fish or leeks and onions', referring to the Pythagorean doctrines which forbade the use of anything that had life for food, connected with the belief in the transmigration of souls. Cp. Sat. 2, 6, 63 *faba Pythagorae cognata*, Juv. 15, 174 *Pythagoras, cunctis animalibus abstinuit qui Tanquam homine, et ventri indulsit non omne legumen.*

22. *utere*, sc. *familiariter* 'associate with'. Cp. Cic. Amicit. 1, § 2 *P. Sulpicio utebare multum.* Cp. 17, 2.

Pompeio Grospho. Ode 2, 16 is addressed to this man, from which we gather that he was a Sicilian, rich, and had held some office either at Rome or in Sicily entitling him to wear the laticlave. There were doubtless many reasons why a rich provincial should wish to stand well with the agent of the great minister Agrippa.

ultro defer 'without hesitation', 'scarcely waiting to be asked'. *Ultro (ultra)* indicates spontaneous action beyond what is demanded, or without waiting for outside pressure.

23. *verum*, see 7, 99. Cp. Cic. Amicit. § 40 *haec igitur lex in amicitia sanciatur ut neque rogemus res turpes nec faciamus rogati.*

24. *annona*, (1) the year's produce, (2) the price of corn, (3) price of anything. 'The price of friendship is low', i.e. true friends do not

make excessive demands on one. *bonis ubi quid deest* 'when the men who make a request are good'.

26—27. *Cantaber...Armenius.*

The *Cantabri* had been frequently in arms during the reign of Augustus, and had proved themselves very formidable enemies. In B.C. 20—19 Agrippa was sent to Spain, and after many difficulties with the disorganised Roman legions, as well as with the warlike Cantabri, succeeded in reducing the country to some order. Dio 52, 11.

Claudi Neronis, see 3, 2. About the same time the king of Armenia, Artaxias, was killed and the country made a Roman dependency, the royal power being given to Artavasdes.

27. *Phraates,* king of Parthia, the 15th of the Arsacidae, had been driven out of his kingdom, B.C. 30—29, and Tiridates put in his place. He was soon afterwards restored [see Od. 2, 2, 17 where the character of Phraates as the most wicked of the Arsacidae gives special point to the lines], when Tiridates fled to Augustus carrying with him a son of Phraates. The Emperor restored him on condition of receiving back the standards taken when Crassus was killed in B.C. 52. These standards were not however given back till B.C. 20; and it is this triumph, which however was one of Roman diplomacy rather than of arms, to which Horace refers here and in 18, 56.

28. *genibus minor* 'on his knees'. The expression is metaphorical, as Phraates had no personal interview with Augustus.

29. *Copia cornu,* cp. Od. 1, 17, 14 *hinc tibi Copia Manabit ad plenum benigno Ruris honorum opulenta cornu. Copia* is personified as the goddess of abundance, of which a horn is the emblem. *Italiae* dat. of the recipient.

EPISTLE XIII.

[This letter affects to be addressed to one Vinius Asella, or Asina, to whom the poet intrusts his book to be conveyed to Augustus, begging him to take a favourable moment for bringing it before him. He playfully pretends to think it a heavy and fragile burden and one which requires great care.]

2. *reddes,* the future as a polite imperative, see 10, 44.
signata i.e. in its sealed *capsa,* see 20, 3.
4. *studio nostri* 'from zeal on my behalf'.
5. *sedulus* 'too importunate'.

6. *uret* 'shall gall'. Cp. 10, 43.

7—8. *quam quo...clitellas* 'rather than at the place (i.e. Rome) whither your orders are to carry your pack'. *ferus inpingas* 'you cast it down roughly in your impatience'. The poet all along speaks playfully of his little volume as though it were a heavy burden, and of the road from his farm to Rome as though it were beset with difficulties and dangers.

Asinae. Orelli holds that Horace uses this word for convenience for the real name Asella.

9. *fabula* 'a bye-word'. Epode 11, 8 *Fabula quanta fui.* Propert. 4, 25 *risus eram.* For *fabula* = 'scandal', cp. Ovid Tr. 4, 10, 67 *Nomine sub nostro fabula nulla fuit.*

10. *uteris*, for the fut. see on l. 2. *lamas* 'marshes' [*lac-ma*].

12. *sic positum...ne portes*, 'arranged in such a way that you should not be carrying it like a rustic carrying a lamb'.

14. *Pyrria*, according to the Scholiast, is a character in a play of Titinius, a drunken maidservant who having stolen some wool carried it in such a way as to be easily detected.

15. *ut...tribulis* 'as some countryman asked to dinner (as being of the same tribe) comes carrying his cap and shoes'. The *soleae* are the indoor shoes or sandals which a guest would wear indoors, though while lying at table they were taken off by the slaves. See Sat. 2, 8, 77. Plin. Ep. 9, 17 *soleas poscit.* The *calceus* was properly the outdoor shoe, but seems to have been worn indoors also. *pilleolus* dim. of *pileus* or *pilea*, 'a small skull-cap' worn apparently even indoors at festivals, especially at the Saturnalia, see Mart. 14, 1, 2.

tribulis 'a fellow-tribesman' asked to a dinner at some festival. For electioneering purposes a man would often take pains to secure popularity in his tribe by invitations, places at the theatre etc., see Cic. pro Planc. § 47; pro Mur. § 73.

16. *ne volgo narres* 'don't tell everyone you meet'. *Ne* with the present subjunctive in prohibitions addressed to definite persons is rare except in the comic poets. Cp. Sat. 2, 3, 88 *ne sis mihi patruus.* Only once in Cicero and then in quoting a proverb, Att. 9, 18. In general prohibitions it is more common, cp. Cic. Sen. § 33 *isto bono utare dum adsit; cum absit ne requiras.* See R. 1600, note.

17. *quae possint* 'such as can'. The subjunctive for a double reason, see 4, 3.

18. *porro* 'straight on': cf. Livy 9, 2 *ire porro.*

EPISTLE XIV.

[Addressed to the steward of the poet's Sabine farm, who longs to be in Rome, while the Poet being detained in Rome longs to be in the country. He therefore expounds the true principles of contentment.]

1. *mihi me reddentis* 'which restores me to physical and mental health': cp. 16, 13—15.

2. *quinque...focis* 'by five householders', coloni or tenants on Horace's estate.

3. *quinque...patres.* We do not know enough of the local government referred to here to decide exactly what Horace means. The Scholiast says that they were *decuriones* i.e. members of the municipal council of Varia; Orelli ridicules this and says that they only attended the markets at Varia and voted at the election of the *duumviri iuri dicundo*, or local magistrates. The point seems to be, as Orelli puts it, 'You a slave are in charge of an estate farmed by five freemen, and yet you presume to be discontented'. *Varia*, a small town eight miles beyond Tibur, now *Vicovaro.*

5. *res* 'circumstance'. Cp. 1, 19, 'whether Horace is master of circumstances, or circumstances of him', i. e. whether he can hold up against adverse circumstances or allows them to affect him too much. Others however take it to mean, 'Let us see whether I pluck the thorns of passion from the mind better than you do the real briars from the field; and whether therefore Horace or his property (which you have the care of) is in the better state'. It seems to me that this use of *res* for a farm is forced and unnatural.

6. *Lamiae pietas* 'the natural sorrow of Lamia who is mourning his brother'. L. Aelius Lamia, to whom are addressed Odes 1, 26, 3, 17, was the son of a rich Eques, L. Aelius Lamia, Consul in A.D. 3, *praefectus urbi* under Tiberius, and died in A.D. 33.

8. *istuc*, to my country estate where you are.

9. *spatiis...claustra*, a metaphor from the race-course. The *claustra* are the barriers or *carceres* behind which the chariots were placed before the start. *Spatia* is 'the course'.

10. *rure*, see 7, 1.

12. *locum* 'the situation' which is not the cause of this discontent.

13. *se non effugit,* cp. Od. 2, 16, 19 *patriae quis exul se quoque fugit?*

14. *tu mediastinus* 'You, when you were a slave in a humble position in town'. The *mediastini* were a lower class of slaves (*vulgares*), doing all kinds of common work. See Becker's *Gallus,* pp. 215, 216. *tacita prece* 'with a silent prayer', not venturing openly to express your discontent. Cp. Pers. 2, 5 *At bona pars procerum tacita libavit acerra,* opposed to *aperto voto. rura petebas* 'you desired to be sent to the country': although it was generally a punishment to a slave to be transferred from the *familia urbana* to the *familia rustica.* See Sat. 2, 7, 117.

15. *ludi et balnea,* the luxuries of the city, see 1, 91; 7, 59.

20. *amoena* 'lovely', 'picturesque'. [Rt. *am. am-o.*]

21. *uncta popina* 'the reeking cook-shop'. Cp. 15, 44; 17, 12.

22, 23. *et quod...uva* 'and the fact that that corner of ground which you occupy will sooner grow pepper and frankincense (the products of the East) than grapes': i.e. that you cannot grow grapes on my small property. The vilicus is supposed to speak of the property contemptuously as a mere *angulus.* Cp. Pers. 6, 13 *securus et angulus ille Vicini nostro quia pinguior.* Cp. 16, 2.

25. *quae possit,* cp. 13, 17.

26. *terrae gravis* 'with a heavy thump upon the ground', like a burly countryman.

et tamen urgues 'and yet, as you discontentedly say, you are always working the fields'. Cp. Verg. G. 1, 99 *Exercetque frequens tellurem atque imperat arvis.*

28. *disiunctum* 'when unyoked'. *strictis frondibus* 'with leaves (of poplar, elm, or oak) pulled off the trees'. Verg. Ecl. 9, 60 *hic, ubi densas Agricolae stringunt frondes.*

30. *multa mole* 'with many an embankment'.

31. *concentum* 'our agreement', lit. 'our singing in unison'.

32. *tenues togae* 'togas made of wool with the nap taken off' opposed to *crassae* Sat. 1, 3, 15. *nitidi,* that is, steeped in unguents in preparation for a feast, cp. Od. 1, 5, 9 *Nunc decet aut viridi nitidum caput impedire myrto Aut flore.*

33. *immunem* 'without making her any presents', cp. Od. 4, 12, 22 *non ego te meis Immunem meditor tingere poculis. Cinara,* probably a fictitious name, but probably also referring to some well-known woman, cp. 7, 28. She is called *bona* [= 'disinterested' as far as

Horace was concerned. See Ter. Hautont. 388, where *bonae* are contrasted with mercenary women] in Od. 4, 1, 4; and from Od. 4, 1, 22 seems to have been now dead.

34. *bibulum* 'fond of drinking'. *media de luce* 'beginning at midday', cp. *media de nocte* 7, 88: *de nocte* 2, 32. The ordinary dinner hour was about 3 p.m., and drinking before that was considered great dissipation. Cp. 5, 8: see Cic. Phil. 2, § 104.

36. *nec...ludum* 'nor am I ashamed of having had my fling, but should be so not to put an end to such dissipations at the proper time of life'; for *ludus* is only *tempestivus* for boys, Ep. 2, 2, 142.

37. *obliquo oculo* 'with jealous eye', the opposite of *oculo irretorto* of Od. 2, 2, 23.

38. *odio...venenat* 'attack me with covert hate and venomous bite'. Od. 4, 3, 16 *Et iam dente minus mordeor invido.* Horace seems to be speaking genuinely of illnatured criticisms both of his writings and his intercourse with Maecenas and Augustus. See Sat. 2, 1.

39. *rident* 'laugh at': so in a somewhat different sense with acc. of person in Od. 3, 16, 5 *Si non Acrisium...Iuppiter et Venus Risissent.*

40. *diaria* 'daily allowance of food', though from Mart. 11, 109 it would seem that a daily allowance of money was sometimes given instead.

rodere 'to gnaw', implying that the food was hard and coarse.

41. *usum lignorum*, see on 12, 4.

42. *calo* 'a low drudge', who has not your privileges. *calo* is used of soldiers' servants in Sat. 1, 2, 44; of grooms, Sat. 1, 6, 102; of rustic slaves apparently in Pers. 5, 95.

43. *ephippia* 'saddle-cloths'. *piger* 'slow', and so unfitted for *ephippia*. But others remove the comma and join *piger* to *caballus*. Ploughing was done in Italy almost entirely by oxen, as to a great extent it still is. Thus in Georgic 3, 49 Vergil, in giving rules for the breeding of stock and horses, seems not to contemplate the use of the latter for the plough at all, *Seu quis, Olympiacae miratus praemia palmae, Pascit equos, seu quis fortes ad aratra iuvencos.*

caballus [the origin of so many high-sounding words in modern languages, 'cheval', 'cavalry', 'chivalry', 'cavalier'] meant properly an inferior riding-horse or pack-horse. Cp. 7, 88; 18, 36: but it is used also for a 'carriage-horse' as better than a mule, Sat. 1, 6, 103, and for a superior riding-horse, Sat. 1, 6, 59.

44. *quam scit*, etc. A Greek proverb thus expressed by Aristophanes [Vesp. 1431] ἔρδοι τις ἣν ἕκαστος εἰδείη τέχνην. The converse of it is expressed by Persius (5, 99) *Publica lex hominum naturaque continet hoc fas, Ut teneat vetitos inscitia debilis actus.*

libens exerceat 'let him be satisfied in exercising'.

censebo 'will be my verdict'.

EPISTLE XV.

[A letter addressed to C. Numonius Vala, who had an estate near Velia and Salernum, asking information about those places, as the poet has been forbidden Baiae by his doctor. He pretends to go only where the best food is to be got, and to intend to become a regular gourmand.]

1. *Veliae...Salerni.* The town of Salernum, mod. Salerno, is in the northern corner of the Bay of Paestum, about twenty miles above that town; Elea or Velia about fifteen miles farther south of Paestum, mod. Alento. Both places were in more exposed positions than that of the sheltered Baiae, and were probably therefore more bracing.

2. *quorum...via* 'what sort of people are the natives and what kind of a road is there?' *Baias*, see 1, 83.

3. *Musa Antonius.* The order of names is reversed for the sake of the verse, as is not unfrequent in poetry, cp. 2, 1. [For instances see Ovid Fast. 2, 500; 6, 723—4; Martial, 1, 113, 5; 8, 3, 16; 8, 3, 5—6; Pers. 5, 73. Nor is it unknown in prose, see Sallust Jug. 27; Tacitus, Agric. 2.] *Antonius Musa* was a well-known physician, whose statue was placed close to that of Aesculapius in honour of his successful treatment of Augustus [Suet. Aug. 51]. He prescribed a cold water cure for the Emperor's liver complaint instead of the usual hot fomentations etc. [Suet. Aug. 81], and he has here ordered the poet a more bracing treatment than the fashionable hot baths.

supervacuas sc. *facit* 'asserts to be of no benefit to me', so Od. 2, 20, 24 *supervacuos honores sepulcri*, 'vain'.

3, 4. *et tamen...invisum*, the emphasis is on *me*, 'and though it is the doctor who prevents my going to Baiae, yet it is with *me* that Baiae is made angry at its desertion'.

6. *dictaque...sulfura* 'and its sulphur baths said to drive the lingering disease from the nerves'. The hot sulphur and vapour baths

of Baiae are referred to by Statius, Silv. 3, 5, 96, who calls it *vaporiferae*, and Mart. 3, 20, 19 *aestuantes Baias*.

9. *Clusinis* 'of Clusium' in Etruria, the seat of Porsena's kingdom. It was on the R. Clanis and was famous for its wheat and spelt [Mart. 13, 8 *Clusinis pultibus*] and had sulphur springs in its neighbourhood.

Gabios, see 1, 11.   Its cold springs are noticed by Strabo.

10. *deversoria*, the road-side inns on the way to Baiae.   *Cumae* is about 6 miles from Baiae.

12. *laeva stomachosus habena* 'showing his anger by pulling the left rein', or 'pulling the left rein angrily'.

14. *utrum...pascat*, this and the previous and following subjunctives depend upon *scribere* in v. 25.

15. *perennes* 'unfailing'.

17. *quidvis* 'any sort of wine', however harsh or rough.

18. *ad mare...veni* 'to the seaside', cp. 7, 11.

lene 'mellow', cp. Od. 3, 29, 2 *Non ante verso lene merum cado*.

19, 20. *cum spe divite*, cp. 5, 17.   *quod...manet...ministret*, see on 13, 17.

21. *iuvenem* 'like a young man '.

22. *apros*.   Lucania, in which Velia was, was famous for its boars, see Sat. 2, 8, 6.

23. *echinos* 'sea-urchins', found on this shore, cp. Sat. 2, 4, 33.

24. *Phaeax* 'a regular Phaeacian', one of the courtiers of Alcinous, see 2, 28.

25. *adcredere* 'trust to you fully': for this rare form cp. *addubites* Sat. 1, 4, 125; *addocet* 5, 18; *adbibe* 2, 67; *adcisis* Sat. 2, 2, 114; *adcrevit* Sat. 1, 6, 26; *adrasum* 7, 50.

26. *Maenius*, a fictitious name.

27. *fortiter*, ironical 'with spirit', i.e. by living a gay life.

urbanus 'a man about town', 'a professed wit', see 9, 11.   Cp. Mart. 1, 42, where a would-be wit of this sort is warned *Non cuicunque datum est habere nasum*.

28. *scurra vagus* 'a wit on the loose', i.e. ready to dine anywhere, having no fixed table at which he was always welcome as a *certus conviva*, see 7, 75.   Cp. 58.

For *scurra* see 18, 2.

29. That is, if he were in want of a dinner he was not particular whether his host were a Roman or a foreigner however much a public enemy.

30. *opprobria fingere* ' to invent derogatory tales ': so *fingere verba* Sall. J. 14; *fingere voltus* Ter. Haut. 887; *fingere crimina* Ov. Her. 12, 177.

saevus fingere, a favourite use of the adject. with prolative infinitive in Horace, imitated from the Greek, cp. 17, 47; *blandus ducere* Od. 1, 12, 11; *piger ferre laborem* S. 1, 4, 12; R. 1361.

31. *macelli* ' of the fish and meat market '. Maenius is ' a plague, whirlwind and whirlpool' of the market because of his enormous appetite. Or. quotes Plaut. Capt. 4, 4, 3 *clades, calamitas, intemperies modo in nostram advenit domum.*

32. *quaesierat,* had ' gained ' by his sharp tongue. Cp. 7, 57.

33. *fautoribus et timidis* ' those who favoured him for the sake of his wit or feared him on account of his malevolence '.

34. *cenabat,* for the construction of *cenare* with accus. see 5, 2. *omasi* ' bullock's tripe '.

35. *quod satis esset* ' enough to satisfy '. *vilis et agninae* ' and (dishes) of cheap lamb '.

36. *scilicet ut* ' so that he might have the right forsooth to say '.

lamna candente ' with hot iron', used for inflicting torture. *nepotum,* ' of spendthrifts '; *nepos* is used for a young dissolute man [cp. Epod. 1, 34 *discinctus nepos*; Sat. 1, 1, 22; 2, 3, 225 etc.] just as *patruus* is used for an over harsh or stern elder.

37. *correctus Bestius* ' like Bestius after he had reformed '. For the omission of a conjunction of comparison, see on 2, 41; 3, 34. The point is that the luxurious glutton, when he is ruined and can only get coarse food, affects to cry out on the luxury of the age, as Bestius (whoever he may be) when he was reformed attacked the vices he had left.

[Many modern edd. have *corrector* ' critic', which Lambinus affirmed that he had found in many MSS. The almost unanimous evidence of MSS. however as far as is known is in favour of *correctus*, which makes very good sense. Orelli however says whether Lamb. found the reading *corrector* or not it is the true reading.]

38. *quidquid erat nactus praedae maioris* ' any richer booty than usual that he may have got hold of ': i.e. any richer dinner to which he may have been invited.

39. *verterat...cinerem* ' had entirely consumed ', as a conqueror capturing a city. Cp. Od. 3. 3, 18 *Ilion, Ilion Fatalis incestusque iudex Et mulier peregrina vertit In pulverem.*

40. *comedunt* ' spend on the table ', with the idea of greedy

'gobbling up', cp. 7, 19. But it was a common expression, see Juv.
1, 138 *una comedunt patrimonia mensa*; and passages quoted by
Mayor ad loc.

42. *hic* 'just such an one'. Cp. 6, 40.

44. *unctius*. Cp. 14, 21; 17, 12.

46. *conspicitur...villis* 'makes a show by being invested in
splendid country-houses'. Horace nearly always uses *villa* of such
large and luxurious houses. His own house is *villula* (Sat. 2, 3, 10);
and though he once calls it *villa* (Od. 3, 22, 5) it is the only instance
of the word being applied by him to any such house. We may
remember that Sallust (Cat. 12) speaks of the *villae in urbium modum
exaedificatae* of this time. For *nitidis*, of the splendour of wealth, cp.
Sat. 2, 5, 12 *res ubi magna nitet.*

EPISTLE XVI.

[Addressed to Quinctius—perhaps the Quinctius Hirpinus of Ode 2,
11,—describing the position of the poet's farm, its healthiness, and his
happiness in it; and urging his correspondent to live up to his reputation, and trust for happiness to the inner consciousness of rectitude.]

1. *ne perconteris*, cp. 1, 13. *fundus meus* 'my Sabine farm'.

2—3. *an...ulmo*, the various elements of Italian country indus-
try, agriculture, olives, orchards, pasture, vineyards. From 14, 23 it
appears that the poet's estate had no vineyards, at least of any value.

ulmo, see 7, 84.

5. Horace speaks of the farm as being *in reducta valle*, Od. 1, 17,
17.

6—7. As you approach the farm you walk Northwards, the East
on your right and the West on your left. *vaporet* Orelli thinks refers
to the mists of evening rather than to the heat of the setting sun.

8. *temperiem* 'the moderate nature of its temperature', neither too
cold nor too hot.

quid? used rhetorically to introduce a new point, 'again'.

8—9. *rubicunda...ferant.* The cornels are grafted and bear both
plums and cornel berries [i.e. wild cherries]: Verg. G. 2, 34 *prunis
lapidosa rubescere corna.* Or as some explain 'the hedges are red with
cornels and sloes'.

10. *pecus* 'the herd of swine', fed on the acorns. Verg. G. 2,
520 *glande sues laeti redeunt.*

11. *Tarentum*, see 1, 45.

12. *fons...idoneus* 'a spring large enough to be called a river', the *Digentia*, see 18, 104. Though some hold that the *fons* refers to *Bandusia* of Od. 3, 13, of which however the position is uncertain.

Thracam...Hebrus, see 2, 3.

14. *utilis* 'wholesome', 'medicinal'.

15. *amoenae*, see 14, 20. *et, iam si credis* 'and if you will believe it after my description'. Bentl. for *etiam*.

16. *Septembribus horis*, see on 7, 5.

17. *audis* 'you are reputed'. For *audire* 'to be called', cp. 7, 38; Sat. 2, 6, 20 *seu Iane libentius audis*; hence 'to have a reputation', Ter. Hecyr. 600 *volgus quod male audit mulierum*.

19. *plus quam tibi* 'rather than to your own conscience'. Cp. Pers. 1, 7 *nec te quaesiveris extra*.

20. *neve* 'or should think anyone but the wise and good happy'. The Stoic doctrine that the *summum bonum* was Virtue, which consisted in following nature, see 1, 106 and 10, 12.

21. Cp. 7, 3.

22—3. 'Don't conceal your fever and dine as if you were well'. The whole passage is imitated by Persius, 3, 94—102. *unctis* 'greasy' with taking up food. The verses of Ovid quoted by Orelli are the best commentary, A. A. 3, 755 *Carpe cibos digitis ; est quidam gustus edendi : Ora nec immunda tota perunge manu.* Cp. also Mart. 5, 78, 6 *Ponetur digitis tenendus unctis Nigra cauliculus virens patella.* The only implements apparently used at table were two kinds of spoons called *cochlea* and *ligula*. See Becker's *Gallus* p. 477—8.

24. *pudor malus* 'a false shame', *mauvaise honte*.

27—29. *tene...Iuppiter*, these are the words of the imaginary flatterer. If you were addressed in such words, says Horace, would you not see at once that they did not apply to you, but could only properly be said of Augustus, and therefore take no pleasure in them?

28. *servet in ambiguo* 'keep doubtful', 'never put to the test', i.e. by bringing you or the State into danger.

30. *emendatus* 'faultless', lit. 'corrected of faults'.

31. *sodes*, see 1, 62. *nempe* 'why of course', cp. 10, 22. This is the answer to Horace's question.

32. *ego ac tu* ' I as well as you'.

33. *qui*, i.e. the public.

34. *fasces*, cp. 6, 53.

36. *idem*, sc. the people. *furem*, sc. *me esse.*

37. *laqueo...paternum*, the worst possible crime, parricide, cp. Od. 2, 13, 5 *Illum et parentis crediderim sui Fregisse cervicem.* For *laqueo*, cp. Sat. 2, 3, 131 *Cum laqueo uxorem interimis.*

38. *mordear, mutem*, deliberative subjunctives. 'Am I to be stung?' 'am I to change?' *mutemque colores* 'Am I to change from white to red, and red to white?' Cp. Propert. 1, 15, 39 *multos pallere colores.*

40. *mendosum* [opposed to *emendatus*, v. 30]=*vitiosum* 'unsound': cp. Pers. 3, 22 *sonat vitium percussa.*

41. The three sources of Roman jurisprudence, decrees of the senate, 'laws' passed by the people, principles settled by judicial decrees.

42. *quo...lites*, i.e. who is often chosen arbiter to decide legal points in dispute. *secantur* 'are decided', cp. Sat. 1, 10, 14 *ridiculum acri Fortius et melius magnas plerumque secat res* (Or.).

43. *sponsore* 'as a security', cp. Pers. 5, 79 *Marco spondente recusas Credere tu nummos.* Cic. Att. 1, 10 *Tulliola tuum munusculum flagitat et me ut sponsorem appellat.*

tenentur 'are gained', 'successfully pleaded', cp. Cic. pro Caecin. 67 *et hoc loco Scaevolam dixisti causam apud Centumviros non tenuisse.*

44. *vicinia tota* 'all his neighbours', representing public opinion, as in 17, 62; and Sat. 2, 5, 106 *Egregie factum laudet vicinia.* Pers. 4, 46 *egregium cum me vicinia dicat, Non credam?*

45. *introrsum...pelle*, cp. Sat. 2, 1, 64 *pellem, nitidus qua quisque per ora Cederet introrsum turpis.* Pers. 3, 30 *te intus et in cute novi.*

47. *ureris.* Cp. 10, 43 and Epode 4, 3 *Ibericis peruste funibus latus.*

49. *Sabellus*, i.e. Horace, who calls himself *Sabellus* [=*Sabinus*] because of his Sabine farm. The Sabelli from whom the Sabines sprang [Sat. 2, 1, 36] were believed to have been a hardy and warlike race; hence Horace speaks of them as types of ancient simplicity and manliness. See Od. 3, 6, 37 *Sed rusticorum mascula militum Proles, Sabellis docta ligonibus Versare glebas.* By calling himself 'Sabellus' he means to pose as a representative of the old simplicity.

50—1. *cautus enim.* 'No', says the moralist, 'as a wolf or a hawk avoid snares, so the cautious animal avoids open danger. But their *natures* are none the better for that'.

52—3. *oderunt...poenae.* This is the distinction; you may abstain from vice for fear; if so you are not *bonus et frugi.*

53. *admittes in te* 'you commit', 'you allow yourself to do'. This expression is commonly used to mark crimes of special iniquity. Cp. Cic. Phil. 2, § 47 *ea in te admisisti quae a verecundo inimico audire non posses.*

54. *miscebis sacra profanis* 'you will be restrained by no consideration of conscience or religion': cp. Sall. Cat. 11 of the corrupted Roman, *sacra profanaque omnia polluere.*

55—6. *unum*, sc. *modium.* *mihi* 'in my eyes', 'according to my philosophy'. Horace makes the very just remark that it is the dishonest intention and not the amount of the theft which constitutes the crime. But he also is thinking of the Stoic doctrine of the equality of all sins, which Cicero states in a popular form in the pro Mur. § 61 *dicunt (Stoici) omnia peccata esse paria: omne delictum scelus esse nefarium, nec minus delinquere eum qui gallum gallinaceum, cum opus non fuerit, quam eum qui patrem suffocaverit.*

58. *vel porco vel bove.* Tellus was worshipped by the sacrifice of a sow as the emblem of fertility: cp. Ep. 2, 139 *Agricolae prisci... Tellurem porco, Silvanum lacte piabant.*

59—60. Imitated by Persius 2, 8 '*Mens bona, fama, fides*',—*haec clare et ut audiat hospes; Illa sibi introrsum et sub lingua murmurat:* '*O si Ebulliat patruus, praeclarum funus!*' *et* '*O si Sub rastro crepet argenti mihi seria dextro Hercule!*'

Laverna 'goddess of thieves'. She is said to have had a temple in the Via Salaria.

63. So much for hypocrisy. But avarice too is a slavery.

qui, see 6, 42.

64. *ob assem* 'to pick up a copper in the street': cp. Pers. 5, 111 (one of the signs of freedom) *Inque luto fixum possis transcendere nummum?* It appears to have been a common illustration used by Sophists. The point seems to consist in the dirtiness of the piece of money rolled in the mud and dung of the street.

65. *cupiet, metuet*, see 2, 51. *porro* 'to proceed'.

66. *mihi*, cp. l. 56.

67. *perdidit arma*, cp. Cic. pro Mur. § 45 *iacet, diffidit, abiecit hastam.*

68. *in augenda re*, cp. 7, 71. *obruitur* 'is entirely absorbed'.

69. Such a man is in fact a slave; you may treat him as a commander does a captive,—sell him for some useful purpose rather than kill him. The ancients (whether truly or falsely) derived the word

servus from *servare*, because a captive kept alive (*servatus*) for sale was the earliest form of slave.

72. *annonae prosit* 'let him be used in transporting corn into Italy'. For *annona*, see 12, 24.

penus, all kinds of provisions.

73. *vir bonus.* If the man has any virtue in him he will be none the less free for such treatment; he will be able to speak as loftily as Dionysus did to Pentheus, king of Thebes, who threatened to imprison him for introducing the Bacchic rites. The remaining dialogue is taken loosely from the Bacchae of Euripides 492 sq. Dionysus is brought before Pentheus a prisoner:

'*D.* Tell me your sentence. What will you inflict?
P. Thy soft luxuriant tresses first I'll shear.
D. My locks are sacred, dedicate to the god.
P. Next give me here thy thyrsus from thy hands.
D. Thyself may take it: that too is the god's.
P. In prison dungeon I will coop thy limbs.
D. The god himself will loose me when I will.'

75. *nempe* 'you mean forsooth', cp. l. 31.

79. *hoc sentit* 'his feeling is this'. *ultima linea*, referring to the *alba linea* from which the chariots in the circus started and at which they finished the race. This *linea* was called also the *calx*, hence *ad calcem pervenire* meant 'to die': cp. Cic. de Am. 101 *optandum est ut cum aequalibus possis, quibuscum tanquam e carceribus emissus sis, cum isdem ad calcem, ut dicitur, pervenire.* See also de Sen. § 83.

EPISTLE XVII.

[Addressed to an unknown person named Scaeva, said by the Scholiast to be an eques. This and the next Epistle are on the same subject,—the bearing which it becomes a man to adopt towards the great, whose patronage he seeks. Horace warns Scaeva that the service of a patron involves some loss of comfort and some self-denial; but insists that, though success in the pursuit is not the highest achievement, yet it is worth something.]

1. *quamvis...consulis* 'though you are quite capable of instructing yourself'. Cicero appears never to use *quamvis* with the indicative, always with concessive subjunctive. But the indicative is used in

the poets freely with this distinction,—with indic. it means 'though as a fact' [cp. 14, 6; Od. 1, 28, 13; 3, 8, 26; 3, 10, 16; Sat. 1, 3, 12; 2, 5, 15; Ep. 1, 14, 6; A. P. 355]: with the subj. it means 'though', 'even if', as a concession or supposition. Cp. these two lines of Vergil, Ecl. 1, 48 *tua rura manebunt...quamvis lapis omnia nudus Limosoque palus obducat pascua iunco* and Aen. 5, 542 *quamvis solus avem caelo deiecit ab alto.* [For *quamvis* with subj. in Hor. see Od. 1, 15, 13; 3, 11, 17; 4, 2, 39; 4, 6, 7; Sat. 1, 3, 15; 2, 4, 90; Ep. 2, 2, 13.]

2. *uti* 'associate with', cp. 12, 22. *maioribus* 'great men', cp. Pers. 3, 92 *de maiore domo.*

3. *quae censet* 'the opinion of', not 'what is the opinion' which would have been *censeat.*

amiculus, playful and affectionate diminutive.

5. *proprium fecisse* 'to make your own'. The perf. infin. is used to describe an action complete and ready, R. 1371. It seems especially frequent after verbs of wishing and striving. Cp. A. P. 168 *Commisisse cavet quod mox mutare laboret.* Od. 3, 4, 52 *tendentes opaco Pelion inposuisse Olympo.*

6. *primam somnus in horam* 'sleep lasting till seven in the morning', which you can't have if you are to get up early to wait on your patron. Cp. Mart. 4, 8 *Prima salutantes atque altera proterit hora.* 1, 55, 6 *et matutinum portat ineptus Ave.* See also Juv. 3, 126.

7. *strepitusque rotarum,* cp. Od. 3, 29, 11 *Omitte mirari beatae Fumum et opes strepitumque Romae.* The noise of Rome at night from the passage of carts is referred to in Juv. 3, 236 *redarum transitus arto Vicorum inflexu et stantis convicia mandrae Eripiunt somnum.* Cp. Hor. Ep. 2, 2, 70—4.

8. *caupona,* see 11, 12; he means the noise of some neighbouring tavern. *Ferentinum,* a lonely mountain village of the Hernici, 48 miles from Rome, on the Via Lavicana.

10. *fefellit,* cp. 18, 103.

12. *siccus ad unctum* 'an unfed to a well-fed man' i.e. 'a poor man to a rich one'. For *unctus,* see 15, 44.

13. *pranderet olus* 'to dine on a dish of vegetables': for constr. cp. 5, 2. *uti,* see v. 2.

14. *Aristippus,* see 1, 18. It was the boast of this philosopher that he was equally at home in every condition of life, and could extract enjoyment from all circumstances. He lived some time at the court of the elder Dionysius, whom he offended by the freedom of

9—2

his remarks, and whose insults he prided himself on treating with calmness.

15. *notat* 'blames'; cp. Sat. 1, 3, 24 *Stultus et improbus hic amor est dignusque notari.*

16. *iunior* 'as being my junior'.

18. *eludebat* 'parried', a metaphor from the gladiators' school. *ut aiunt*, cp. 7, 49.

19. *scurror...mihi* 'I play the parasite for my own advantage, you to gain the applause of the people by your show of austerity'. *hoc* 'this way of mine'.

equus...rex, Orelli quotes a Greek proverb ἵππος με φέρει, βασιλεύς με τρέφει. For *rex* cp. 7, 37.

21. *officium facio* 'I pay my court'. Thus the social duties of calling etc. are called *officia urbana* Mart. 1, 56, 14; and the book sent to pay court to its author's patron is addressed as *officiose* id. 1, 71, 2. Cp. supr. 7, 8.

verum es 'still though you ask for things of little value (i.e. bare necessaries) you thereby put yourself under an obligation and in an inferior position to the donor, as well as I to the great man whom I ask for more expensive things'. [Orelli reads *vilia rerum*, but the all but unanimous evidence is for *verums*, and in my opinion the latter makes the better sense.]

22. *fers te* 'you boast', 'you give yourself out'.

nullius, masc. 'of no one' (Or.).

23. *color* 'condition of life'. Cp. 18, 4; Sat. 2, 1, 60 *Quisquis erit vitae color.*

25. *duplici panno* 'with a rag wrapped twice round him', instead of a chlamys and tunic or χιτών. This was called by the Cynics a διπλοῦς (Or.).

26. *decebit* 'will sit well on him'. *mirabor si* 'whether', R. 1754.

29. *feret* 'will sustain'. *personam* 'a character' as in a play, properly 'a mask'. *non inconcinnus* 'not without a certain grace'. Cp. 18, 6.

30. *Mileti textam...chlamydem* 'a chlamys woven at Miletus'. The Milesian wool was famous, and purple dyes were much used there. Cp. Verg. G. 3, 306 *quamvis Milesia magno Vellera mutentur Tyrios incocta colores*. Id. 4, 334 *eam circum Milesia vellera nymphae Carpebant, hyali saturo fucata colore*. Mart. 8, 28 (to a *toga*) *nec Miletus erat vellere digna tuo.*

angui 'worse than a snake', cp. Od. 1, 8, 8 *cur olivum Sanguine viperino cautius vitat?* For the abl. *angui* cp. *igni, colli, imbri, navi, tussi,* and see Munro on Lucr. 1, 978. The oldest form of the abl. of i-stems was *īd*: then *ē*: then from about B.C. 150 *-ei* or *-ī*, e.g. *fontei, omnei* and *luci, vesperi.* Afterwards the *ĕ* became most common, but the *-ī* survived in many words as above.

31. *chlamydem,* see 6, 44.

32. *sine vivat ineptus* 'let him live like the fool he is'.

34. *attingit solium Iovis* 'is a happiness nearly divine': cp. 1, 1, 6 *terrarum dominos evehit ad Deos*: id. 36 *Sublimi feriam sidera vertice.*

caelestia 'immortality'.

36. *non cuivis.* This is a translation of a Greek proverb, οὐ παντὸς ἀνδρὸς εἰς Κόρινθον ἔσθ' ὁ πλοῦς: but what the origin of it may be is somewhat doubtful. Two explanations have been suggested, (1) that Corinth being a rich, extravagant and immoral town it is not everyone that can afford to go there; (2) the difficulty of sailing there makes it not an ordinary feat to reach Corinth. It is one of those proverbs which have become so completely a part of all literature and with so definite a meaning, that it has almost ceased to matter what their origin may have been. The point here seems to be 'what we seek may not be worth much, but it takes some trouble to attain, and is not in everyone's power'.

37. *sedit = cessavit* 'has played the poltroon'. *succederet* impersonal.

38. *fecitne viriliter?* 'can he be said to have acted a part worthy of a brave man?' 'Can we call his achievement an act of courage?'

39. *hic est.* The question is all contained in this 'was it an act of courage', i.e. a virtuous act.

quod quaerimus 'the question we are investigating', i.e. whether such an achievement is or is not praiseworthy. Imitated by Pers. 5, 174.

41—2. *virtus nomen inane.* Cp. 6, 31. Horace's view seems to be 'The cultivation of the great presents difficulty, in so far as a man faces and overcomes that difficulty he is performing an act of 'virtue' though possibly not the highest', περὶ δὲ τὸ χαλεπώτερον ἀεὶ καὶ τέχνη γίνεται καὶ ἀρετή [Aristot. Eth. Nic. 1, 3].

experiens 'it is the man who tries that has a right to demand'.

43—62. The poet, dismissing the question whether it is worth while or no, proceeds to give some practical rules.

rege, see 7, 37.

44. *pudenter*, cp. 7, 37 *Saepe verecundum laudasti*.

45. *hoc*, i.e. that you should get some advantage from your patron.

47. *pascere firmus*, see on 15, 30.

49. *findetur.* The result will be, says the poet, that the bounty will be divided. For *quadra* 'a quarter' of a dish cp. *quadra placentae sectae* Mart. 3, 77, 3. For its use here cp. Juv. 5, 2 *Ut bona summa potes aliena vivere quadra.* *dividuo* 'divided', lit. 'which can be divided'.

52. *Brundisium* 'to Brundisium', as Horace was himself taken by Maecenas, see Sat. 1, 5. The modern Brindisi, the port for Greece, and to which the Via Appia was extended from Capua.

Surrentum, mod. *Sorento*, on the Bay of Naples, where many Romans had villas. Its wine is referred to in Sat. 2, 4, 55. For *amoenum* see 14, 20.

54. *cistam* 'a basket' for carrying clothes etc. Cp. Ovid, Met. 2, 554 *texta de vimine cista* ; probably borne by a porter, *cistiferus*, Mart. 5, 17 ; in Juv. 3, 206 it is filled with books.

viatica 'all the necessaries of travel'.

55. *catellam* 'a little chain' [dim. of *catena*] or a little dog as some think [*catulus*].

56. *periscelidem* 'a bangle for the ancle' [περὶ σκέλος].

59. *plănus* 'a cheat', lit. 'a wanderer' πλάνος. The number and variety of beggars feigning various maladies and misfortunes seems to have been as great at Rome in these as in the present times. See A. P. 20; Juv. 14, 302 ; Pers. 1, 89; 6, 32.

60. *Osirim*, the man swears by Osiris because he is or pretends to be an Egyptian, a foreigner appealing more to pity; or because of the superstition of the people being particularly at that time directed to the worship of Isis and Osiris.

62. *peregrinum*, some one who doesn't know the tricks of the streets. *vicinia*, see 16, 44. *rauca* 'noisy' (the meaning of 'hoarse with shouting' need not be pressed): cp. Juv. 8, 59 *exultat rauco victoria circo.*

EPISTLE XVIII.

[Another Epistle on the same subject as the former, the rules to be observed in associating with a Patron, addressed to the same person as Epistle 2. These maxims are briefly these: 5—20 not to mistake rudeness and an affectation of roughness for manly independence: 21—36 not to vie with your rich patron in extravagance: 37—8 to keep his secrets: 39—66 not to run counter to his wishes unnecessarily: 67—71 to be careful what you say of others: 76—88 to be specially cautious whom you introduce to him: 89—95 to be cheerful and companionable: 96—112 but amidst all these cares not to neglect study and philosophy. Comparing these exhortations with Epistle 2, we may conclude that Horace is addressing somewhat ironically a young man, fairly embarked in a life of society, with some tendencies to culture, which Horace thinks it necessary or worth while to encourage.]

1. *liberrime.* Orelli rightly sees in this epithet a hint to Lollius not to be too free spoken.

2. *scurrantis*, see 17, 19. The *scurra* is both a joker and a cause or subject of jokes.

4. *discolor* 'unlike in her whole course of life'. Cp. *color* 17, 23.

6—8. *agrestis*, as opposed to *facetus*, see 6, 55. *inconcinna gravisque* 'ungraceful and offensive', see 17, 29.

tonsa cute 'with hair cropped close to his head'.

8. *mera libertas* 'unalloyed independence'. Pers. 5, 82 (in a rather different sense) *haec mera libertas! hoc nobis pilea donant!*

9. *virtus est medium.* The doctrine of the old Academy and of Aristotle ἀρετὴ μεσότης δύο κακιῶν. Cic. de clar. § 149 *omnis virtus, ut vetus Academia dixit, mediocritas.*

10—11. *imi derisor lecti.* The *imus lectus* was the couch on the right hand of the table (looking down it). At the corner nearest the *medius lectus* the host generally reclined with his chief guest at the corner seat of the *medius lectus.* The two lower places on the *imus lectus* were the less honourable places and were usually assigned to the dependent, or *scurrae*; as in the dinner given by the vulgar rich man described in Sat. 2, 8, though the other guests follow the lead of Vibidius in punishing the host's wine—*imi Convivae lecti nihilum nocuere lagoenis* (40). The wine was passed not from this place but from the *summus in summo* the last place on the opposite couch. See Cic. de Sen. § 46. *derisor=scurra* 'the professional joker', asked for the express purpose of making fun, and perhaps leading the laugh at his patron's jokes, as is described in the A. P. 427 sq. and Persius, 1, 53 sq.

12. *verba cadentia tollit*, catches up the chance words of his patron, which are falling flat, and calls attention to them.

13. *saevo magistro*, his master who is fond of the rod, *plagosus* [Ep. 2, 1, 70]. *dictata*; cp. 1, 55.

14. *reddere* 'repeat'. *partes secundas* 'a second-rate part', such as is played generally by a parasite whose business it is to reecho his patron's words. As the parasite in Ter. Eun. 2, 2, 1

> 'If one says 'no',
> I answer 'no': if 'yes', I answer 'yes':
> In fine I've laid this task upon myself
> To echo all that's said.'

15. *de lana...caprina* 'about goat's wool', i.e. 'about nothing'. So the Greek ἐς ὄνου πόκας [Arist. Ran. 186] and the English 'pigeons' milk'.

16. *propugnat...armatus* 'he defends opinions on trifling subjects with all the paraphernalia of logic'.

scilicet, ut non 'am I not then, forsooth, to hold truth of the first importance, and speak out boldly what I sincerely think?' 'To think that I shouldn't etc.'

18. *pretium...aetas* 'I would not barter my sincerity for a second life'. *sordet* 'is insufficient', 'is despised', cp. 11, 4.

19. *ambigitur quid enim* 'well, after all, what is the point in dispute?' *Castor* and *Docilis* are two gladiators. *plus sciat* 'is the more scientific fighter'.

20. *Minuci...Appi.* For the *via Appia* see 6, 26. The *via Minucia* is not accurately known. From Cic. Att. 9, 6—where some cohorts are said to have started from Alba, which Prof. Wilkins shows to be Alba Fucentia, by the *via Minucia* for Brundisium,—it would seem to have led to that town by a route farther inland and probably somewhat shorter than the *via Appia*, but more difficult and mountainous. Even which of the Minucii gave his name to the *porta Minucia* is uncertain. See Palmer on Sat. 1, 5, 6.

21. *praeceps alea* 'ruinous dice'. Gambling was forbidden by law except during the Saturnalia and some other festivals; but it nevertheless went on in secret, and according to Suetonius [Aug. 71] Augustus himself was an eager gambler.

22. *unguit*, for the use of expensive unguents see Od. 2, 7, 8; 2, 3, 13; 2, 7, 23; 3, 14, 17; A. P. 374. The *unguentarius* is among the tribe of harpies who crowd round the young heir, Sat. 2, 3, 227.

23. *inportuna* 'restless', insatiable': cp. Sat. 2, 5, 96 *Importunus amat laudari.*

25. *decem vitiis instructior* 'furnished with ten (= many) more vices'. For this use of *instructus* of character cp. Ter. Haut. 451 *ad perniciem instructa.*

26. *regit* 'assumes to direct' or 'school'. Thus the professor says, Cic. pr. Mur. 60, *non multa peccas, sed si peccas regere te possum.*

28—9. *meae stultitiam patiuntur opes* 'I am wealthy enough to afford to play the fool'. So Catiline (Sall. Cat. 20) says of the nobles *omnibus modis pecuniam trahunt vexant; tamen summa libidine divitias vincere nequeunt.*

30. *arta toga* 'a scanty toga', not a fine and flowing one. Cp. *toga brevis* Mart. 11, 57, 6. See on 14, 32. *comitem=clientem,* cf. Pers. 1, 54 *scis comitem horridulum trita donare lacerna.*

31. *Eutrapelus.* This refers to P. Volumnius Eutrapelus, a friend of Antony, Atticus, and Cicero. He was a noted wit. Cicero [Fam. 7, 33] thanks him for his witty letters, making a pun on his name and the Greek εὐτραπελία, and says that he is the only rival in wit whom he fears.

34. *dormiet in lucem,* see 17, 6.

35. *nummos alienos pascet* 'he will feed borrowed money', i.e. he will swell the wealth of the usurer and his own indebtedness by paying high interest. Thus Persius (5, 150) says of a money-lender that he *nutrierat nummos quincunce modesto,* 'had nursed his money'. *nummos alienos* is equivalent to the usual *aes alienum.*

36. *Thraex,* i.e. a gladiator, a class of men that often came from Thrace and other northern countries. See Sat. 2, 6, 44.

37. Don't pry into the great man's secrets or divulge them when you know them.

38. *vino tortus et ira* 'though put to the question by wine and anger, and so tempted to speak'. See 2. 37; A. P. 434 *torquere mero.* Plin. Ep. 9, 21 *torqueris enim cum tam lenis irasceris.*

40. *ille,* the patron.

41—2. Amphion and Zethus, twin brothers, were sons of Zeus and Antiope. Amphion devoted himself to the lyre given him by the Muses or Apollo, while Zethus hunted and tended the flocks; until Zethus induced his brother to lay aside his lyre and take up arms.

42. *suspecta severo* 'disliked by his more earnest brother'. *Severus* is opposed to the easy playful character associated with the lyre. So *tragoedia* is *severa*, Od. 2, 1, 9; and what are becoming to a *severus* are *seria dictu*, A. P. 107.

44. *moribus*, sc. *severis*.

46. *Aetolis plagis* 'nets' made for catching boars like those of the Aetolian Meleager. See 6, 58, sq.

47. *inhumanae* 'morose'. *Camenae*, see 1, 1. *senium* represents the worst side of old age, querulousness, moroseness and ill-temper. Hence it is used for 'moroseness', without reference to age. See Cic. de Sen. § 7 *moderati enim et nec difficiles nec inhumani senes tolerabilem senectutem agunt; importunitas autem et inhumanitas omni aetati molesta est.*

48. *cenes pulmenta* 'dine on viands': for constr. see 5, 2. *pariter*, 'with your patron'. *pulmenta* = ὄψον, anything eaten with bread.

laboribus empta 'which you have earned by your labours in the hunting field'; with a reference to the 'sauce of fatigue', which gave a flavour to the black broth at Sparta; cp. Sat. 2, 2, 20 *tu pulmentaria quaere sudando.*

49. *utile famae* 'good for a man's reputation', as a manly youth, see Od. 3, 13, 10. Though Cicero makes Cato speak of hunting and fowling as mere amusements, *supervacanei operis*, de Sen. § 56.

53. *non est qui tractet* 'there is no one who can handle'. The subjunctive is required in such a clause as being indefinite: cp. *sunt qui.*

coronae 'of the ring of spectators'. So Mart. 1, 42, 6 *otiosa corona.* In the same sense of the spectators in the campus, see A. P. 38 *ne spissae risum tollant impune coronae.*

55. *militiam puer*, i.e. you received a manly training in arms as became a Roman, cp. Od. 3, 2, 2 *Robustus acri militia puer Condiscat. Cantabrica*, not the expedition referred to in 12, 6, but an earlier one in B.C. 26—25.

56. *duce*, i.e. Augustus. *Parthorum signa refigit* 'has caused the arms (taken in B.C. 52, when Crassus was killed) to be taken down from the Parthian temples' and restored to Rome. See 12, 28. Horace refers to this triumph of Augustus again in Od. 4, 15, 4 *tua, Caesar, aetas...signa nostro restituit Iovi Derepta Parthorum superbis Postibus.*

58—66. Horace has been just dilating on the reasonableness of Lollius humouring his patron's taste for hunting, especially as he is such an adept at that and other athletic and hardy sports, that it can be no trouble to him. He then goes on to say: 'Yes, and I may add, to dissuade you from staying away from him without good excuse, you are not always staying away for serious employments, but are at times merely amusing yourself with playing a game at sea-fighting on your pond at home'.

58. *ac ne te retrahas* '(I say this) lest you should withdraw and keep away without good excuse'.

59. *quamvis* 'though it is true that you do nothing unbecoming and extravagant'. So Ep. 2, 2, 144 *verae numerosque modosque ediscere vitae.* For *quamvis* see 17, 1.

60. *nugaris* 'you engage in light amusements'. Cp. Sat. 2, 1, 73 *nugari et discincti ludere.*

62—64. A sham naval battle in mimicry of the battle of Actium (B.C. 31) which Lollius is supposed to be enacting in his lake at home. Such sham naval combats were becoming the fashion, and Augustus gave a public exhibition of this kind in an artificial lake on the banks of the Tiber [Suet. Aug. 43].

62. *refertur* 'is represented'.

64. *velox victoria* 'swift (or 'winged') Victory'. This may be best understood by observing the figure of Victory so often found on Roman coins,—a winged figure bearing in one hand a laurel-wreathed caduceus, in the other holding out a chaplet of leaves.

65—66. If you seem to your patron to sympathise in his tastes he will be ready to applaud yours.

utroque pollice. As in the gladiatorial games the people expressed their appreciation of the combatants, and their wish that they should be saved, by pressing down the thumb *laudare pollice* = 'to applaud', *utroque pollice* 'with both thumbs' is only 'to applaud emphatically'.

67. *protinus* 'next', in a series of subjects, cp. Vergil G. 4, 1 *Protinus aerii mellis caelestia dona Exsequar.*

siquid 'if at all', εἴ τι.

69. *percontatorem,* a line quoted by Sir P. Sidney in his 'Apology' as one of those which when once read is never forgotten.

71. *inrevocabile verbum,* expressed again in A. P. 390 *nescit vox missa reverti.*

77. *aliena peccata* 'another's faults', i.e. those of a man you have introduced.

78. *tradimus* 'introduce': see 913.

79. *deceptus omitte tueri* 'when you find yourself deceived about his character don't try to back up' the man you recommended. *omitte*

used like *noli* with infinitive to form a prohibition, cp. Od. 3, 29, 11 *Omitte mirari beatae Fumum et opes strepitumque Romae.*

80.   *ut* 'that by showing your honesty in disapproving real faults you may have the greater influence in defending a friend when innocent'.

crimina (false) 'accusations'.

penitus notum 'thoroughly known'.   So Od. 1, 21, 4 *penitus dilecta.* Pers. 3, 30 *te intus et in cute novi.*

82.   *dente Theonino* 'by an envious malignity like that of Theon'. We do not know who Theon was: Porphyrion says that he was 'a man of that time *rabiosae dicacitatis*'.   The attack of malignant jealousy and depreciation is often spoken of under the figure of a bite : cp. Od. 4, 3, 16 *Et iam dente minus mordeor invido.*   Epode 6, 15 *An, siquis atro dente me petiverit.*   So Sat. 1, 4, 8 *absentem qui rodit amicum.*

ecquid = nonne 'Don't you at all perceive that danger will before long come upon you?'

84—5.   *paries proximus* 'the house next door': cp. Verg. Aen. 2, 311 *iam proximus ardet Ucalegon.*

tua res agitur 'your interest is at stake'.

87.   *in alto* 'out at sea', safe from shoals and quicksands.   *mutata* 'a shifting gale': cp. *aura fallax* Od. 1, 5, 11.   *retrorsum* 'backwards' to the dangerous shore.

90.   *agilem,* see 1, 16.

91.   *media de nocte* 'from midnight on'; see 2, 32 and 14, 34. [This line is justly suspected : (1) it is wanting in a large number of MSS.; (2) it seems like an imperfect recollection of 14, 34; (3) there is a difficulty in deciding whether *bibuli* belongs to *Falerni* or *potores*: with the former it is superfluous, with the latter perhaps unmeaning: (4) speaking of drinking *media de nocte* transcends all bounds of ordinary Roman habits, and such excess is not in point here.   Bentley boldly altered to *liquidi* and *de luce*, which certainly is a better verse.   By cutting out the words bracketed in the text a good sense would be obtained.]

92.   *porrecta* 'held out' by the patron when he has first drunk himself from it, and then passed it on to the person he names, in imitation of a Greek custom.   See Cic. Tusc. 1, 40 *Graeci enim in conviviis solent nominare cui poculum tradituri sunt.*

93.   *nocturnos tepores* 'the warm air at nights', which to a man heated with wine might bring fever: see Pers. 3, 91 sq. [Orelli against the greater number of MSS. reads *vapores*, quoting *fluctuare vaporibus* *febrium* Apul. Met. 10, 2. Holder retains *tepores*, quoting Sat. 1, 4, 29 *ad eum* (*solem*) *quo Vespertina tepet regio.*]

94. *nubem* 'cloud of gloom'. Eurip. Hipp. 183 ὀφρύων νέφος. Cic. in Pis. § 20 *frontis nubecula.*

95. *obscuri* 'reserved', 'dark', i.e. hiding some possibly dangerous thoughts.

96. *leges*, fut. for imper. see 13, 10. *percontabere* 'question those of your friends who are philosophers'.

97—103. Several questions of ethics of supreme importance on which Lollius should consult the philosophers.

98. *semper inops* 'that is never satisfied', cp. 2, 56 *semper avarus eget.*

99. *num pavor* 'or whether fear and hope for what is of only doubtful advantage agitates and troubles you'. *mediocriter utilia*, the ἀδιάφορα, 'things indifferent', of the Stoics; only virtue and vice, as absolutely good and bad, are to be considered good or bad: other things, such as health, sickness etc. are indifferent, as being merely materials which may be employed for good or evil. Zeller, *Stoics and Epicureans*, p. 218.

100. *virtutem* 'whether virtue is innate or teachable': for a discussion of which point see Plato Meno, and Protag. cc. xi—xxi.

101. *tibi amicum* 'content' or 'satisfied with yourself', i.e. what can give you a clean conscience, cp. 3, 29.

102. *pure* 'absolutely', without leaving any traces of disturbance.

lucellum, a diminutive, expressing contemptuously the yearning of a man for wealth, 'that delightful and darling gain', cp. Sat. 2, 5, 82.

103. *fallentis semita vitae* 'the path of a life led in privacy', 'escaping observation', cp. 17, 10.

104. *Digentia*, see 16, 12.

105. *Mandela*, mod. *Bardela*, a village on the Digentia. *bibit*, cp. Horace's description of the Gaul as *Rhodani potor* Od. 2, 20, 20.

107. *et mihi vivam* 'and may I live for my own true interests', i.e. not for external vanities. Cp. Mart. 1, 49, 41 *Non impudenter vita, quod reliquum est petit, Cum fama quod satis est habet.* [Many MSS. read *ut*, which editors explain to mean 'provided that'. I think that *et* introducing an independent wish is more in Horace's manner. It really amounts to the same thing: 'May I have no more than I have, or even less, and may I (in either case) live to myself'.]

109. *in annum* 'for each recurring year', may the harvest of each year fill my granary with enough for the year, cp. 2, 39; 11, 23.

110. *neu...horae* 'and may I not hover trembling on the turn of each uncertain hour'. Cp. Od. 2, 16, 31 *Et mihi forsan tibi quod negarit Porriget hora.* Ep. 2, 2, 172 *puncto mobilis horae.*

fluitem, cp. Lucr. 3, 1052 *incerto errore fluitans.*

112. *det vitam*, cp. the prayer of Od. 1, 31, in which the *integra mens* is included. *aequus animus* is that content which is unaffected by good or bad fortune alike, see Od. 2, 3.

EPISTLE XIX.

[Addressed to Maecenas, and complaining of those who servilely imitated him (10—34), and secondly of those who unreasonably attacked him (35—49).]

1. *prisco Cratino* 'the old Cratinus', not old in years, but of ancient times. Cratinus a comic poet contemporary with Aristophanes [i.e. circ. 425 B.C.] is joked at for his love of wine in Arist. Pax 700.

3. *aquae potoribus.* The praises of wine are so frequent in Horace that it is hardly necessary to refer this to any one passage. We have already (5, 15 sq.) in these Epistles had one dissertation on the kindly effects of the grape, and the poet had long ago declared that *siccis omnia deus proposuit* (Od. 1, 18, 3).

potoribus, dat. of the agent, rare except with gerundives, passive participles [see 1, 94], and adjectives in *-bilis.* See R. 1146.

ut = ex quo 'since'. Cp. Plaut. Stich. 29 *nam viri nostri domo ut abierunt hic tertiust annus.* Od. 4, 4, 42 *Qui primus alma risit adorea Dirus per urbes Afer ut Italas...equitavit.* R. 1719. So also *cum* is used for *ex quo*, Plaut. Merc. 3, 1, 35 ; Ter. Haut. 54.

4. *adscripsit* 'enrolled poets among the Satyrs and Fauns which attend him'. Cp. Od. 3, 3, 35 *adscribi quietis ordinibus deorum.* For the Satyrs and Fauns attending on Bacchus, see Od. 2, 19, 4. The Faun, Horace says [Od. 2, 17, 29], had especial charge over poets,— *Mercurialium custos virorum.* The Satyrs are represented with human bodies, and goats' legs : the Fauns are human in shape except the ears which are like those of goats.

6. *laudibus vini.* There is no passage perhaps which can be quoted from Homer directly in the praise of wine, but he frequently

describes its use in banquets [e.g. Il. 1, 595 sq.], and its cheering effects, and gives it such epithets as ἡδύς, μελιηδής, μελίφρων, εὔφρων.

arguitur vinosus 'is convicted of being fond of wine'.

7. *Ennius...pater.* Horace calls Ennius [B.C. 239—169] *pater* because of his antiquity, and as the 'father' of Latin poetry. His works were very numerous and of many varieties, Epic, satiric and dramatic. His chief work was an Hexameter poem on the history of Rome, in 18 books, called Annales. Horace is fond of attributing a taste for wine to the ancient sages and heroes, as for instance Cato, Od. 3, 21, 12.

ad arma dicenda 'to describe battles', i.e. in his Annals.

8. *Forum putealque,* i.e. business and a mercantile career. The *puteal Libonis* was an altar in the shape of a well-head near the *Tribunal* in the *Comitium,* under which the whetstone cut by the Augur Attus Naevius was supposed to be buried. The Schol. to Pers. 4, 49 says that it was in the *Porticus Iulia* near the *Arcus Fibianus,* and that money-lenders congregated near it. Porphyrion says that it was the 'seat of the Praetor', who would be trying money cases. A coin of the *gens Scribonia* exists with a representation of the *puteal;* but it is possible that there were more spots than one in the forum called by this name. See Sat. 2, 6, 35. It seems to have been called *puteal Libonis* or *puteal Scribonianum* from having been restored by Scribonius Libo.

9. *siccis* ' to non-drinkers of wine', see on v. 3.

severis, see 18, 42.

10. *hoc simul edixi* 'as soon as I had given out this mandate'. Horace playfully uses the formal legal word like a magistrate issuing an edict, as though he had authority in the republic of letters. He may mean that he said words to this effect in company, or he may refer only to the general tone of his writings. See on v. 3. [Some MSS. have *edixit,* which has also been defended by some Editors. The subject of the verb in that case would be Ennius or Liber. But it introduces a needless difficulty.]

11. *certare* 'to drink against each other at night', i.e. by challenging each other to larger and stronger cups. Sat. 2, 8, 35 *Et calices poscit maiores,* cp. 18, 92. Horace protests against the fashion in S. 2, 6, 68.

12—13. *vultu torvo...exiguae togae,* cp. 18, 30. Philosophers affected the short tunic [τρίβων] instead of the ample toga, and the Stoic Cato made a compromise by reducing the extent of his toga to the lowest.

It is generally assumed that the Cato alluded to is Cato Uticensis
who committed suicide at Utica [B.C. 46], and who was conspicuous
for his rigid adherence to Stoic doctrines, and who seems to have
intentionally aped the manners and appearance of his ancestor Cato
the Censor [B.C. 234—149]. It cannot be settled certainly, but there is
some weight to be attached to the objection that Horace would not be
ready to quote the manners of the great Anti-Caesarian leader with
implied approval, though at an earlier date he might speak of his
nobile letum [Od. 1, 12, 35], which Julius Caesar himself spoke
of with admiration. And the *vultu torvo*, 'grim expression', suits an
epigram on the elder Cato quoted by Plutarch,

'   Red-haired, sharp-toothed, fierce-eyed,—from him gone dead
   E'en Proserpine herself will turn her head'.

vultu...pede...textore, are ablatives which partly express manner,
partly means.

15.   *Iarbitam...aemula* 'The tongue which would rival Timagenes
was the ruin of Iarbita'. Timagenes was a native of Alexandria and
was brought a prisoner by Gabinius (B.C. 55) to Rome, where he taught
Rhetoric. He seems to have been renowned for a freedom of speech
which got him into trouble; and Iarbita—an unknown man, but said by
Porphyrion to have been Cordus a Mauritanian, his name Iarbĭta being
a nickname from Iarbas king of the Gaetulians—may have ruined
himself by a similar free use of his tongue. *rumpit*, used of 'bringing
to confusion' by any violent means, cp. Sat. 1, 3, 135 *Urgueris turba
circum te stante miserque Rumperis*. Thus, as a term of hunting, *rumpere
leporem* 'to run down a hare', Mart. 1, 49, 25.

16.   *urbanus* ' a wit ', cp. 15, 27.

17.   *vitiis imitabile* 'a model which may be copied in its faults', i.e.
which may be apparently followed, but yet only in its weak points : as
for instance the imitations of a fashionable poet, such as Byron, in regard
to dress, hair, and cynical style.

18.   *exsangue* ' which makes pale '.

cuminum, this plant ' cumin ' was believed to produce paleness,
whence Pers. 5, 55 *pallentis grana cumini*.

19.   *servum pecus* ' ye servile herd', cp. Lucan Phars. 6, 152
O famuli turpes, servum pecus. As an adj. *servus* is often found with
homo in Plautus, but with other subjects rarely until the Augustan
period. Cp. Ov. F. 6, 558 *serva manus*. Livy has *servum caput* and
corpus, servae urbes, etc.

21—2. I entered on a new field, viz. that of writing Latin Lyrics in Greek metres. Cp. 3, 11 and notes. His steps are *libera* as not being trammelled by precedents set by others. *per vacuum* 'through a field not occupied by others'. So Horace elsewhere boasts (Od. 4, 9, 3) *Non ante volgatas per artes Verba loquor socianda chordis.* And says (Od. 3, 30, 13) that he was *Princeps Aeolium carmen ad Italos Deduxisse.*

23. *dux* 'as a king-bee', which Vergil [Georg. 4, 67, 187] calls *ductor* and *rex*. For omission of *ut* see 2, 41 ; 3, 34.

23—5. *Parios...Archilochi...Lycamben.* Archilochus of Paros [flor. circ. B.C. 700], the earliest Ionic poet to write regular Iambic verse. The story referred to here is of his attacks upon Lycambes, whose daughter Neobūle had first been promised to him and then refused. He accused the father of perjury, and his daughters of immorality, in a poem which was recited at the festival of Demeter, and so terrified them that the daughters hanged themselves. Cp. Epode 6, 13 *Lycambae spretus infido gener.* A. P. 79 *Archilochum proprio rabies armavit iambo.*

res 'subject matter'.

26. *foliis brevioribus* 'with a poet's crown of shorter leaf', i.e. with a less honourable wreath.

28. *temperat* 'the masculine Sappho forms her muse (=her style) by the metre of Archilochus'. Horace is defending himself for keeping the ancient metres. Sappho, he says, copied the measure of Archilochus though not his matter, as did Alcaeus : why should I not do the same? He refers especially to the Epodes.

pede 'metre'. *mascula Sappho* 'Sappho of a genius worthy of a man'. She was an Aeolian poetess of Mytilene in Lesbos [*Lesboum barbiton*, Od. 1, 1, 34]: flor. circ. B.C. 600.

29. *Alcaeus*, of Mytilene [circ. B.C. 600], one of the earliest Aeolian lyric poets.

ordine 'arrangement'.

30. *quaerit* 'looks out for'. For this and the following line, see note on verse 23.

atris 'venomous' : thus *atro dente* (Epod. 6, 15) of detraction.

31. *famoso* 'defamatory', cf. Sat. 211, 68.

32—3. *hunc*, sc. Alcaeus. *latinus fidicen* 'a Latin lyric poet'. Cp. Od. 4, 3, 22 *monstror digito praetereuntium Romanae fidicen lyrae.*

volgavi 'gave to the public': see on verse 21 ; and cp. Verg. G. 3, 3 *Cetera quae vacuas tenuissent carmine mentes, Omnia iam volgata.*

iuvat inmemorata ' my delight is that with themes such as have
never been sung before I should be read by generous eyes and held by
generous hands'. There is a double sense in *ingenuis* of 'nobly born',
referring to Augustus, Maecenas etc., and ' refined ' ' candid '.

35.   *scire velis* ' would you wish to know? ' *opuscula*, cp. 4, 3.

36.   *premat* 'depreciates'. Cp. Verg. Aen. 11, 401 *ne cessa...
extollere vires Gentis bis victae, contra premere arma Latini.* Cic. in
Pis. 41 *vos meam fortunam deprimitis? Vestram extollitis?*

37.   *ventosae,* see 8, 12.   *venor = capto* 'try to get'.   *tritae vestis* 'by
the present of old worn clothes'.   Persius has imitated this in describing
the patron reading his verses and then asking for candid criticism (1, 53)
*calidum scis ponere sumen, Scis comitem horridulum trita donare lacerna,
Et: 'verum'—inquis—'amo : verum mihi dicite de me'.*

39.   *nobilium scriptorum auditor et ultor* 'I who listen to nobles
reciting their verses and avenge myself by reciting my own'.   This seems
better than taking *ultor* seriously as 'vindicator', 'defender of my
patron's poems'.   Or. aptly quotes Juv. 1, 1 *Semper ego auditor
tantum? nunquamne reponam?*   Such private recitations took place
often after the cena [Mart. 4, 8, 10.   Pers. 1, 30].

40.   *grammaticas tribus* 'the schools of the critics' who recite
and lecture on old poets.   He calls them 'tribes', as though they had to
be canvassed for a poet's reputation as the political tribes for election
to office.

pulpita, to be taken closely with *tribus,* 'the chair' or ' pulpit' from
which these lectures are given.   The two together embrace the whole
scene.

41.   *hinc illae lacrimae,* a proverb taken from Ter. Andr. 126.

spissis theatris ' if I plead that I am ashamed of publicly reciting
verses not good enough for crowded auditories '.   Roman poets gave
recitations of their own works as a means of publication.   An exhaustive
list of references to this custom in Latin literature will be found
in Mayor's note to Juv. 3, 9.   The first Roman poet who is said to have
done this was Pollio after B.C. 39 : but the practice had quickly grown.
Horace refers to his dislike of reciting in Sat. 1, 4, 23 *volgo recitare
timentis.*

nugis addere pondus ' to give an air of importance to trifles '.

43.   *ait* 'says my critic'.   *Iovis,* sc. Augustus.   So Martial of
Domitian (4, 8, 11) *Tunc admitte iocos: gressu timet ire licenti Ad
matutinum nostra Thalia Iovem.*

44. *manare*, transitive, 'that you distil'. *poetica mella*, cp. Persius
·prol. 14 *Cantare Pegaseium nectar.*

45. *ad haec* 'To such an attack I am afraid to answer by sneer'.
naribus uti 'to use the nostrils', i.e. 'to turn up the nose'. Cp. Pers.
1, 40 *rides ait, et nimis uncis Naribus indulges.* Hor. Sat. 1, 6, 5
naso suspendis adunco Ignotos.

46. *formido*, ironical. *acuto ungui* 'detraction', like *dente*, see on
18, 82.

47. *iste locus* 'the place you suggest', i.e. the public recitation
room.

diludia 'intermission', 'truce to this dispute': said by the Scholiasts
to be properly the number of days allowed between exhibitions of
gladiators, during which a gladiator could not be forced to enter the
arena.

48. *ludus*, such a jesting dispute as this which we are maintaining.
The word is suggested by *diludia* above. *genuit*, aorist, see 7, 21, 'is
wont to breed'.

EPISTLE XX.

[This Epistle, which is in the form of an address to his own book, is
added by the poet as an epilogue on collecting the previous letters into
a volume. He playfully anticipates its fate, and gives some particulars
of his personal history. It seems natural that the previous letters
should have been sent at various times to the persons to whom they
were addressed, and finally collected and published when there were
enough of them, just as Ovid did with his letters Ex Ponto. See Pont.
5, 9, 51.]

1. *Vertumnum Ianumque.* Not the Janus of 1, 54, but the temple
of Janus in the Argiletum. The temple of Vertumnus was not far off
in the Vicus Tuscus: and near them were the booksellers' shops
[*tabernae*], or their stalls fixed against pillars [*pilae, columnae*].

spectare 'to be looking longingly towards'.

2. *scilicet*, used in introducing ironically an imaginary speech, see 6,
36.

ut prostes 'that you may be exposed for sale'.

Sosiorum, the brothers Sosii were a firm of booksellers, see A. P.
345.

pumice. The pumice was used to render the edges of the roll smooth. See Mart. 1, 66, 10 *pumicata fronte.* 1, 117, 16 *Rasum pumice purpuraque cultum...Martialem.* 8, 72 *Nondum murice cultus asperoque Morsu pumicis aridi politus...libelle.*

3. *claves et sigilla* 'the keys of the desk [*scrinia*, Mart. 1, 4, 2] and the seals put upon the roll's case' [*capsa*, cp. Ep. 2, 1, 268, of his book going to be sold as waste paper, *capsa porrectus aperta*]. Or perhaps of the store-house chests (*armaria*), Sat. 1, 4, 22; 1, 10, 63. See 13, 2.

4. *paucis*, i.e. to the friend to whom they are addressed, and his immediate intimates to whom he or the poet recites them. *communia* 'publicity'.

5. *non ita nutritus.* Though I never accustomed you to such publicity by reciting you in public.

descendere. This is the usual word for men going from home into the forum or the streets, like our 'to go down town'. Cp. Cic. Phil. 2, § 15 *hodie non descendit Antonius* 'isn't coming to the forum'.

8. *in breve cogi* may best be explained literally, I think, 'crammed into some narrow space', either of the *capsa* or pocket in the folds of the toga or paenula : see Mart. 14, 84 on a *manuale* or wooden case for a book ; *Ne toga barbatos faciat vel paenula libros, Haec. abies chartis tempora longa dabit.* Orelli seems to consider the phrase as = *in angustum cogi*, to be brought to a standstill or difficulty, comparing Ter. Haut. 669 *in angustum nunc meae coguntur copiae.* Professor Wilkins explains both metaphors by the double reference to the scroll as a book and a slave.

plenus = satur.

9. *quod si non desipit* 'If he is a true prophet', cp. εἰ Κάλχας σοφός Soph. Aj. 783. *odio peccantis* 'from anger at your mistake' in wishing for publication.

10. *donec deserat* 'until your novelty is gone': this use of *donec* with subj. is rare. Cp. A. P. 155. See R. 1664.

12. *tineas pasces* 'feed the worms', by being thrust into some box and left there to be devoured by moths and worms as other stuffs— *blattarum ac tinearum epulae* Sat. 2, 3, 119.

inertes 'slow working'. Others explain 'barbarous' = *sine artibus.*

13. *vinctus* 'done up in a parcel and sent to Ilerda', in Spain, mod. *Lerida.* Horace imagines his book getting out of fashion in Rome and taking refuge in Utica (near Carthage) or Spain. This is not all evil, for he elsewhere boasts prophetically that he will be known and read in

Africa, Spain, Gaul, and in the farthest northern provinces, see Od. 2, 20, 13 sq.

15. *male parentem*, disobedient, cp. 19, 3. *in rupes protrusit* 'pushed over the precipice'.

18. *occupet* 'shall come upon you'; cp. 7, 66. *balba senectus* 'a stammering old age' is to come upon the book because in its old age it is to be used for the halting and stammering reading lessons of small boys: it will become in fact a school-book, as Juvenal [7, 226] says Horace had in his time become, *Quot stabant pueri cum totus decolor esset Flaccus, et haereret nigro fuligo Maroni.* Cp. Hor. Sat. 1, 10, 82.

extremis in vicis 'in some back slums'.

19. *cum tibi sol* 'when the warm afternoon has gathered an audience for you'. For after dinner (about 5) was the hour for such private readings, see on 19, 39; and *tepidus* indicates some heat short of midday, see on 10, 15. Some however explain the reference to the schools.

20. *libertino natum*, see Introduction § 1. Sat. 1, 6, 6 sq. A man is *libertus* to his patron, *libertinus* to the rest of the world. *in tenui re* 'humble circumstances'. So Cic. uses *tenues* of men in a humble rank, Mur. § 70.

21. *maiores...extendisse* 'that I have stretched my wings till they are too large for the nest': i.e. I have risen in life higher than my origin gave reason to expect. So in Ep. 2, 2, 40 he describes himself as crippled in means by the loss of his father's estate after Philippi *decisis humilem pennis.* For *nidus = domus*, cp. 10, 6.

23. *primis urbis belli domique* 'the men of first importance in the city both in military and civil services'. He means Augustus, Maecenas, Agrippa, Pollio and others. *placuisse*, cp. 17, 35. Cp. Ter. Adelph. prol. 18 *Eam laudem hic ducit maximam, quom illis placet Qui vobis univorsis et populo placent.*

24. *praecanum*, the usual meaning given to this word is that of 'grey before my time'. But as Horace was now 'forty-four', to be grey would not be sufficiently remarkable to be mentioned as a distinguishing feature, though of course it may mean that he had turned grey early. *Prae* in composition means (1) 'before' in time, (2) 'very', (3) 'in front', 'at the end', as *praeacutus*; and I am inclined to think that Horace means 'grey in front'. Some years before this Horace spoke of his *albescens capillus*, 'turning grey', Od. 3, 14, 25.

solibus aptum 'taking pleasure in sunny weather'. Horace did not like cold, see **7, 10.** 'Taking the sun' was a usual measure for the preservation of health: thus Pliny [Ep. 6, 16] describes his uncle in the ordinary disposition of his day as *sole usus.*

25. *tamen ut=tamen ita ut*, 'and yet placable'. Horace more than once refers to his quick temper in youth [Od. 3, 14, 27; 1, 16, 22 sq.], and was perhaps of the *genus irritabile vatum* [Ep. 2, 2, 102] to the last.

27—8. As Horace was born in the Consulship of L. Manlius Torquatus [B.C. 65] he was 44 in the Consulship of M. Lollius [B.C. 21].

Decembres, used doubtless poetically for *annos* ; still it also refers to the fact that Horace was born in December [the 8th, Sueton. *vit. Horat.*].

collegam duxit, in B.C. 22, Augustus being absent, one of the Consulships was reserved for him, and in B.C. 21, M. Lollius entered on the Consulship alone. Augustus refused the other Consulship, and after some disturbances Q. Aemilius Lepidus was elected. As Lollius was first elected and entered on his office Horace says that he *duxit collegam* ; it is not apparently a technical word indicating any official action. It may be translated 'received as his colleague '. A man whose colleague was appointed by lot might be said *ducere*, and perhaps the word is intentionally used to indicate that Lollius had no part in selecting him, 'it fell to his lot to have as his colleague'. [The reading *dixit*, adopted by several editors, is without MS. authority, and though it is plausibly defended by the fact that a consul elected is sometimes said *dicere collegam*, it does not appear that the phrase meant that there had been an election, as there was in this case; rather that the consul 'nominated' his colleague because of the failure of any regular election. When one consul presided at the election of another he was said *creare*.]

INDEX.

PROPER NAMES.

INDEX II.

To the Notes.

uro 10, 43; 13, 6; 16, 46
urtica 12, 8
usus 12, 4; 14, 41
ut vales? 8, 13
ut = ex quo 19, 3; = ita ut 20, 28; *omitted in comparisons* 2, 41; 3, 34; 15, 37; 19, 23
uti, 'use', 'enjoy', 2, 49; *associate with* 12, 22; 17, 2, 13

valdius 9, 6
valere 2, 49
valetudo 4, 10
venaticus canis 2, 66
venenare 14, 38
venor 19, 37
ventosus 8, 12; 19, 37
verba voces 1, 34; '*mere words*' 6, 31; tollere 18, 12
verecundus 7, 37
vertere in cinerem 15, 39
verum 1, 11; 7, 99; 12, 23
veternum 8, 10
via Appia 6, 26; 18, 20; Minuci *ib.*

viatica 17, 54
vicinae turres 3, 4
vicinia 16, 44; 17, 62
victoria velox 18, 64
villa 15, 46
violens 10, 37
viriliter 17, 38
virtus 1, 41, 52, 53; 2, 18; 17, 41; 18, 9, 100
vitiosa 1, 86
vitium 1, 41; vitiis imitabile 19, 17
vivaria 1, 78
vive vale 6, 67
vivere 10, 7; 18, 107
volgare 19, 32
volgo 13, 16
volpecula 7, 29
volpes 1, 73
votum, venire in, 11, 5
vultus torvus 19, 12

wine, effect of, 5, 16; *praises of,* 19, 3

For EU product safety concerns, contact us at Calle de José Abascal, 56–1°, 28003 Madrid, Spain or eugpsr@cambridge.org.

www.ingramcontent.com/pod-product-compliance
Ingram Content Group UK Ltd.
Pitfield, Milton Keynes, MK11 3LW, UK
UKHW020314140625
459647UK00018B/1873